INTRODUCTION TO PALMISTRY

Know the Significance of Lines of the Palmistry

Author
Dr. Narayan Dutt Shrimali
M.A. Ph-D.

President
Indian Astrological Study & Research Centre
&
Tantra-Mantra-Yantra, Palmistry Institutes of Dreams

Published by:

F-2/16, Ansari Road, Daryaganj, New Delhi-110002
☎ 011-23240026, 011-23240027 • *Fax:* 011-23240028
Email: info@vspublishers.com • *Website:* www.vspublishers.com

Regional Office : Hyderabad
5-1-707/1, Brij Bhawan (Beside Central Bank of India Lane)
Bank Street, Koti, Hyderabad - 500 095
☎ 040-24737290
E-mail: vspublishershyd@gmail.com

Branch Office : Mumbai
Jaywant Industrial Estate, 2nd Floor–222, Tardeo Road
Opposite Sobo Central Mall, Mumbai – 400 034
☎ 022-23510736
E-mail: vspublishersmum@gmail.com

Follow us on:

All books available at **www.vspublishers.com**

© Copyright: V&S Publishers
Edition 2017

The Copyright of this book, as well as all matter contained herein (including illustrations) rests with the Publisher. No person shall copy the name of the book, its title design, matter and illustrations in any form and in any language, totally or partially or in any form. Anybody doing so shall face legal action and will be responsible for damages.

Printed at : Repro Knowledgecast Limited, Thane

PUBLISHER'S NOTE

The study of palmistry was one of the highest-ranked forms of learning in ancient times. This art is said to have flourished in Egypt and among India hundreds of years ago. This form of fortune telling is now seriously studied worldwide and continues to fascinate everyone. And hence our interest in coming out with this book.

People everywhere continue to read their palms and believe that what they learn is true. Whether it is accurate or not is a debatable issue. Take a look down at your hands, notice whether they are fleshy or boney. Are fingers short or long? Are knuckles prominent? Do the fingers look balanced or does one look larger than the others? Palmistry shows us that all of this means something. Each finger and part of the palm tells a part of the story of who you are and the study of palmistry reveals that story. Each line characterizes a different aspect of the future.

The author explains in simple language the method of seeing a Hand. He goes on to tell readers about methods to interpret Hand-Palm, Fingers, Thumb, Mounds, and important lines of Life, Head, Heart, Sun, Fate, Health, Marriage and other secondary lines.

Take a look at your own palm and see if you can match up your lines.

We had been feeling a need for an authoritative book containing important aspects of palmistry with illustrations and digestible information conveyed in a simple language for average readers. We, at V&S Publishers are confident that the author Dr.Narayan Dutt Shrimali has succeeded in putting across the subject matter in a manner that will help readers achieve their learning curiosity.

CONTENTS

Publisher's Note	3
Foreword	7
Introduction	35
Hand : A Study	43
Hand-Palm, Fingers and The Foreparts of Fingers	51
The Thumb and Fingers	60
Mount	76
Pairs of Mounts and Signs on Hand	92
Lines	105
The Life Line	118
Head Line	123
The Heart Line	132
The Sun Line	140
The Fate Line	147
The Health Line	157
The Marriage Line	163
The Secondary(Unimportant) Lines	168
Other Signs in the Hand	179
Determining the Time	193
Procedure of TakingHand-prints	195
The Goddess Panchanguli	198
Practical Knowledge of Palmistry	**206**
Conclusion	**220**

FOREWORD

Palmistry is in itself a complete science which can forecast the future of an individual authentically. Human life has become so complex that it faces many obstacles, difficulties and keen competition to achieve its objective. Under these circumstances, when a person wants to reach his goal, he feels an uncertainty about his future—whether he will achieve his aim or not.

In fact, a person who achieves his aim in his lifetime is to be thanked. Though the goal is just one aim-point do so but thousands of people try to touch this aim-point, only the fortunate ones take a leap and are able to touch it.

If the future of the person is open before him, then it becomes easy for him to reach his destination. He can conveniently do so by adopting and selecting such paths which successfully lead him to his destination. For this purpose, we need services of such a science which can allow foresee and understand one's future course.

All the sciences of the world are able to indicate facts or results of the past, but palmistry, is the only science which tells us about the complete past as well as the future. Astrology has been called as the *'Third Eye'* because the ordinary man can see with his two eyes but an astrologer has the 'third eye' by virtue of which he can also look into the future of a person with such ease as he can see the present moment.

Astrology is fully authentic and fact-finding science in itself. Its results are also fully certain and clear and the facts established by it are certain like the facts of other sciences. Astrology is not such a science that it makes clear the life of a person from minute to minute but it is meaningful in this way that it tells about the events of the life of a person and forecasts about the coming events or circumstances in the life of that person.

Astrology has many branches. Palmistry is important and authentic because its results are clear. In the other branches of Astrology, the moment of the birth of a person has a very important role to play and if the moment of birth is not fully sure, then there will be difference in the results of the forecasts. But in palmistry, the moment of the birth of a person is not so important, instead the lines and marks on the palm of a person are of vital importance to his life.

Serious researches on palmistry have started in the world and today even the scientists are compelled to believe that through palmistry, all those incidents which will occur in the life of a person in future, can be known beforehand.

In today's family life, palmistry is considered very important because the small, thick, thin and oblique lines in the palm of a person have the whole future imprinted there. One does not require the calculations of mathematics nor does one need to know the exact time of birth of a person. It is also a fact that the creator of these lines, the Almighty God, is fully authentic and, as such, there is no possibility of any error. What one requires is an expert and authentic palmist so that he can know the incidents easily.

Palmistry has contributed a good deal to the science of medicines. The greatest and most famous physician of the world is today compelled to believe that the disease of a person can surely and certainly be recognised even by observing the palm, its colour and lines thereon, whereas it takes two to three days to find out the disease of a person through medical equipment and aids and these two or three days may prove to be fatal for the patient. But through palmistry, it can be known within a few seconds where and what sort of ailment is there in the body of a person and how it can be removed.

All the sciences have now recognised the importance of palmistry and it is felt that, to attain completeness in life, one has to rely on palmistry. One can know and recognise the future time before one passes through it.

This science is greatly developed in India. Our ancestors had studied it thoroughly. The rules propounded by them are authentic. If one studies this science on the basis of indications, then the results will be fully authentic. Our old sages have clearly indicated that the whole life of a person and even every minute of the life of a person can be known through the lines on the palm.

But gradually, this science was left into oblivion and the number of those who could pursue it through study dwindled. Along with it, it no longer remained a science but it turned itself into an institution of religion and a profession to earn livelihood. The result was that this science did not have the necessary depth and very few actually knew it.

But even today, in India, there are many such monks and learned persons who have full knowledge of this science. They have deep study, labour and self-thought in this science. They have devoted every moment of their lives in the progress of this science. Their only desire is that this science should attain its full development. This should be useful for the welfare of the world and it should guide the path of the world.

"I do not claim to be an authority in this field but I have devoted more than sixty years of my life for the progress and study of this science. I have felt that in India, there are still many sages, monks and learned persons who have a full and complete knowledge of this science and who can give shape to the past, the future and the present moments."

"I have spent most of my time in the caves of the Himalayas. I have lived quite close to nature and have been searching for those monks who have studied this science thoroughly well, and whose very words are authentic—I am wonderstruck that they have limitless knowledge about this science and they can be called full authorities on Palmistry."

"I have lived with Yogi Sahajanand, who is the best devotee and an authority in the field of Palmistry. It is a known fact throughout India that he is the most authentic monk in this field. He has studied this subject seriously and the conclusions drawn by him in this field are milestones in it. During a conversation, he said that palmistry was a science and the whole life of a person could be drawn by seeing the lines on his palm. But the completeness in this field could only be achieved if the palmist had the 'desired knowledge'. By desired knowledge, he meant communion with a deity, by virtue of which he could be authentic. He meant to suggest that the palmist should have communion with his favourite deity or he should have mastered *Panchanguli* by his worshipping along with his knowledge about palmistry, then only he could be matchless in the field."

"Worshipping *Panchanguli* is the best devotion for a palmist. If one gains devotion and favour of this deity, one can achieve completeness in the field. Yogi Sahajanand remarked that he had read it in the holy scriptures that devotion of Goddess *Panchanguli* is the best and most essential for palmists but he himself could not perform this devotion and it had remained an unfulfilled desire of his life."

"When I wanted to know if he knew any learned man or monk who had complete knowledge of palmistry and who had also mastered Goddess *Panchanguli*, without hesitation he told me the name of Dr. Shrimali. This name was quite unknown to me because I had spent most of my life in the caves of the Himalayas. I have tried to master exorcism and I consider myself to be a student in the field of palmistry. I have a great love for this science and am nearly mad after this science. I want mastery over this science so I am in search of a person who is fully competent in this field."

"When I heard the name of Dr. Shrimali from Swami Sahajanand, I at once made inquiries about Dr. Shrimali, viz., where he lived and what sort of a monk he was."

"Swamiji told me that though Dr. Shrimali had lived as a monk but at present, he was a householder and had established the Indian Astrological Study and Research Centre at Jodhpur. Whatever work he had done was matchless in itself. He had alone done so much work which even many institutions could not have done jointly. My claim to achieve perfection would be unmeaningful till I had met him."

"Then and there I decided to go to Jodhpur. Though I did not know his address, yet I thought that the person, who was matchless in the field and whose fame had reached the monks and ascetics living far away in the Himalayas, would certainly be a known personality to the inhabitants of that city (being a V.I.P.) and it would not be difficult to locate him or his residence."

"Though I decided to go to Jodhpur very soon, I kept busy in many other works and though I tried to go earlier, I couldn't go for the next two months but during this period whomsoever, monk or ascetic I met, I inquired about Dr. Shrimali and all of them agreed univocally that Dr. Shrimali was the most authentic palmist of the present times. His work in the field of palmistry was rare. The standards set by him in this field were authentic. He had given rare knowledge through his books after latest research to the present generation."

"On my wandering spree, I reached Haridwar. There I met Swami Anjani Nandan. He is an important personality there and the whole of the Northern India respects him."

"His words are considered authentic because he is an objective person. His words are devoid of flattery and deceit. When I informed him that I was eager to see Dr. Shrimali and told him that he was considered an authority in palmistry, he at once permitted me and replied that I would be fortunate if I could gain something after meeting Dr. Shrimali. I could know many things regarding Dr. Shrimali from him because Swamiji had practised and perfected certain charms with Shrimaliji. Along with it, Swamiji had also gained much knowledge about palmistry from Shrimaliji."

"I stayed in the hermitage of Swami Anjani Nandan for a week and during this period, we talked about Shrimaliji nearly daily and this talk about him encouraged my self-confidence and I became very eager to meet Shrimaliji, whatever be the circumstances."

"I asked Swamiji (Anjani Nandanji is thus called by the people there) if I would be able to learn something from him. Then Swamiji told me that he had lived in the company of Shrimaliji for nearly eight months and whatever he could learn about Shrimaliji was that he was not able to assess the depth of knowledge of Shrimaliji. The more closer he went to Shrimaliji, the greater did his personality evolve. His name was considered respectful and authentic in the field of Astrology. He was also matchless in exorcism, yoga etc. He couldn't be compared with anyone."

"He had spent most of his life for the progress and perfection of astrology. He had only one desire—the only dream—that this science should achieve perfection and was recognised as the best science in the world. Keeping in view this object, he had established the Indian Astrological Study and Research Centre through which this science could be perfected and such enthusiastic youths be prepared who might achieve success in this field."

"Swamiji further said that it was easy to meet him but it was difficult to get his favour because he did not like any sort of laziness nor any avoidance. He gave a hard test to one, who wanted to be his pupil and one who got success in the test would find the doors of progress open for him. Swamiji told that he himself had to struggle hard to gain Shrimaliji's favour. "I tried everyday but did not get success." said Swamiji. I used to consider myself important in Northern India and thought that when my name was famous in itself. As soon as I reach there, he will favour me and I shall be able to gain knowledge from him easily. But when I reached there, all my convictions went with the wind. I found that he knew my name and he had knowledge about me and he gave me so much love and respect that I have not forgotten it even today. But so far as the question of gaining knowledge was concerned, he was strict in his dealings. Shrimaliji told me that love and affection were altogether different things and that respect shown to me was his duty and my service was his religion but when I wanted to enter the field of devotion, I was just an ordinary pupil and if there was laziness in the work and life of a pupil, he would not gain perfection and if I did not attain perfection even after being his pupil, it would be considered a shortcoming in the personality of Shrimaliji. So he kept some control on his pupils so that they might attain perfection in the least time."

Swamiji continued, "I tried my level best to be his able pupil. I had thought myself perfect and I felt that I could labour hard but when I found him persevering, I felt myself a pigmy before him. I found that every moment spent by him was useful and full of activity. His every moment was valuable. The hard labour put in by him is not possible for us. But it becomes a glaring example before us that we should also be ready to put in labour like him."

Swamiji continued, "I could win his favour almost after two months or I can say that I had experienced the feelings of studentship. The moment I could pass his test, which was a valuable one in my life because whatever I could gain from him after that moment, is a treasure of my life and whatever perfection is felt today, is all due to his kindness."

In our discourse, Swamiji told me many anecdotes and told me that those events took place before him or before such persons who were considered authentic and important in the society. I listened to many anecdotes from Swamiji. Some of these are being given in the following lines:

Once a civilized gentleman inquired from me if Dr. Shrimali was at home.

The person was looking quite civilized and had come in a taxi. He was asked to sit in the drawing room. After sometime, Dr. Shrimali met him in my presence. He was taken aback as soon as he saw his hand.

The newcomer said that he was a famous businessman from Gorakhpur and had come there by air to discuss about his trade.

Dr. Shrimali said, "Don't tell lies. You don't mean what you say. But you are quite afraid to the core of your heart because you killed your rival hardly ten days ago and hence, you have run away from there. You are not thinking about your business at the moment but you want to know if there would be any trouble for you in the near future."

The face of the newcomer turned white and he began to stammer and he asked the same thing from Shrimaliji which Shrimaliji had told him.

Dr. Shrimali said, "The indication connected with murder has fully bulged out on your thumb and there cannot be two opinions that you will be arrested within a week from today and exactly three years after, you will be hanged."

The newcomer could not withstand the bitter truth told by Punditji. He started trembling. He could hardly stand on his feet. He went out of the drawing room immediately and sat in the car frustrated, without saluting anybody.

After some days, it was known through newspapers that he had been arrested at Patna.

I stood surprised on the personality of Dr. Shrimali because such a bare, naked truth could only be told by a person who had full faith in his words and who had perfect knowledge.

Once Punditji was sitting in his chamber and I was learning some facts about Palmistry. That day a meeting was scheduled with a central leader. He rang up that he had reached Jodhpur and was about to come to see him in a few minutes. Punditji permitted him to come.

After sometime, a long and white car stood before his house and a brilliant person, clad in white garments, came out. He was an important leader in the centre and had come to meet Punditji for some of his particular problems. He came and sat in Punditji's chamber and I went out of it.

For sometime, Punditji and the central leader remained busy in their talks. When I came out, I saw a poor, old beggar, having an aluminium bowl containing a few coins, standing at the gate. When he saw me, he requested me to give him *chapatis* to eat. I went inside the house and brought two *chapatis* with a little curry and gave it to him. He sat outside the chamber and began to eat.

Nearly after 20-25 minutes, Punditji opened the door of his chamber and the beggar stood up and spread his hand before Punditji for alms. The beggar requested him to give him some coins so that he might have something to eat.

The central leader was ready to go out. Out of courtesy, Punditji came to the gate to see him off. When he saw the spread hand of the beggar, he was startled and at once caught the beggar's hand and asked him who he was and where he had come from.

The leader and I were surprised why Punditji had caught the beggar's hand when he was to be dismissed after being given a coin or two.

The beggar replied, "I am a poor man and I got something to eat at your door. I demand ten or five paisa from you. You are well-off, so if you can give me some money, I shall consider it my luck."

Shrimaliji smiled and said, "Your hand is spread before me and the lines on it reveal that you are not a beggar but you are a high officer at present. You should be quite prosperous economically. Your present countenance is a deceit and artificiality. Your Sun line clearly indicates that you are a high officer in the spy branch."

The beggar at once snatched his hand and turned to go away but I intervened his going away. He confessed that he was a central intelligence officer and had been deputed to know fully well about the central leader. He also confessed that he had taped the conversation held between the leader and Punditji by means of his equipment.

Punditji asked him to come and sit in his room. Feeling defeated, he told everything about himself and put on the tape which he had taped outside, for the listeners.

The leader was perplexed. His experienced eyes could not detect what Shrimaliji had detected through the lines. He at once said, "Shrimaliji, you are really very great. There is none to match you in the knowledge of palmistry. Whatever you have brought to light through the lines of the palm, is before me. I am quite experienced, yet I could not recognise this beggar, whereas you have found out his true identity in a moment through his palm."

When Punditji asked, the intelligence officer removed the conversation, passed between him and the central leader and wishing respectfully, he went out.

I am an evidence to this and have even started feeling after this event that in the field of palmistry, Punditji is unique and he can't be compared easily.

His favourite pupil also told us about an event. Once Punditji had stayed in a famous hotel of Delhi and the news of his arrival in Delhi had been published in the dailies.

It was at about noon that a foreign lady came to see Punditji. She was speaking English very fluently. Her dress was ordinary and she was showing poverty, misery and trouble through her eyes.

She entered the room and told Punditji that she had heard his name in U.S.A. and she had desired to meet Punditji in India at Jodhpur but all her luggage had been stolen and she didn't have a single coin with herself.

When she read the news in an English daily about the arrival of Punditji to Delhi, she couldn't resist and without taking prior permission from Punditji, she had come down to meet him. She said, "I do not want to know anything else except this one thing that I was born in a poor family and have withstood poverty and misery throughout my life but I have a desire to be a rich but I don't see any such circumstances."

She continued, "At this moment, when all my luggage has been stolen, I have become beggarly for even single coins. I have not had anything to eat for the last three days." Saying this, she spread both of her hands before Punditji.

Punditji saw the lines on the palms for a minute or two, then he saw her face which was an embodiment of poverty and misery. Her eyes were exhibiting the troubles and tears of poverty.

For another second, Punditji looked into her palms and he became sure in his heart. He had a hearty laugh. He put away both of her hands and said, "Madam, don't deceive me. You are not poor but a multi-millionaire even at the moment. You are also not hungry. You took your dinner in a five-star hotel only yesterday evening. You don't lack anything even here."

"The way your mount of Venus and its corresponding line are developed make you a successful actress and its authenticity is before me. The way you have acted can cheat even very experienced persons but my knowledge can't be cheated that way. You are a perfect actress and you do not lack anything concerning money and fame."

Hearing these words, the actress fell at the feet of Punditji and she confessed that she was really a film actress from Hollywood and was a multi-millionaire. She had come to India to attend a film festival. She had heard the good name of Punditji but from that day, she began to believe it firmly that Punditji was unique in palmistry. She became grateful and emotional and began to weep. She drenched Punditji's feet by her tears.

She asked many questions regarding her future life, Punditji replied courteously all her queries. She went to her country and gave statements to newspapers and magazines. Her first and foremost statement was that her best achievement in her visit to India was her meeting with a rare personality on palmistry.

Once three persons came to see Punditji at Jodhpur from Indore. Two of them were males and third was a female. I was sitting near Punditji at that time. It was morning. Punditji had just come to his office after performing his morning chores of bathing and worshipping, when the three persons entered and told that they had come all the way from Indore to meet Punditji.

One of the men introduced himself as a government officer and the woman was his wife. They didn't have any issue. They had come there to know if they would ever be bestowed with the happiness of a son or not.

Then he introduced the person who had come with him and said that he was his fast and trustworthy friend, Mr. Kumar. He was a succesful doctor and that he had full faith on the doctor but the doctor had no faith in astrology. He (the doctor) considered astrology as tomfoolery. He (the officer) had brought the doctor to remove his false convictions about astrology.

Punditji listened his talk peacefully and then said, "If he has no faith in astrology or palmistry, then let it be so. Why do you compel him to believe it?"

At once, Mr. Kumar interrupted, "It is all a fraud. It has no reality. All the astrologers or palmists of the world cheat to grind their own axe."

Punditji remained peaceful and said, "You have no authority to comment till you meet an authentic person in these sciences. This science is fully authentic in itself. It is something else that you did not meet someone who could give you an authenticated result. So you could not believe it."

Mr. Kumar said, "A lie and deceit is always a lie and deceit. So I cannot be convinced with such talks."

Shrimaliji became angry on his impertinence and said, "Inspite of your being a doctor, you are uncivilized. When you do not know even the basics of this science, how dare you criticise this science in this way? I don't tolerate such uncivilized manners."

But Mr. Kumar was in very high spirits. He spread his hand before Punditji and said, "if you can tell me any authentic event of the past two or three days about me, I shall be your slave throughout my life."

Punditji looked into the open palm of Mr. Kumar and said, "I shall tell you the event clearly but it will be difficult for you to bear it, so it is better I don't say anything."

But Kumar did not keep quiet and spoke, "I don't find any particular knowledge in you also, so you are only side-tracking by your words."

For the first time, I saw anger on the face of Punditji. He said, "Mr. Kumar, you are an uncivilized animal and unfaithful friend. This gentleman has termed you as his friend but you are a blemish on the name of friendship because only this morning, you have had an intercourse with the wife of your friend and this love affair is continuing for the last 6 years. Your friend doesn't know it. When your friend had gone out for a walk this morning, you had an intercourse, with his wife and to prove it, you can still find the drops of semen on her saree. She has not changed her saree after that."

All the three were at their wit's end to hear this. The face of Mr. Kumar turned red as if someone had slapped him on his face.

Punditji said, "The line on your palm is making clear this fact. This event took place only two hours ago. I did not want to tell you people all this but your unfaithful personality compelled me to tell you all this. If you desire, I may call a lady doctor and prove the authenticity of this event."

The third person was at his wit's end and could not believe that his wife and his friend could play such a big fraud with him. The whole atmosphere turned very heavy for nearly two minutes but Kumar's face was evidently telling that whatever Punditji had told was true to every word.

I saw that Kumar and the woman went out quickly and also saw the third person following them nervously.

The face of Punditji was still red-hot with anger. He took some minutes to cool down. After cooling down, he said, "I do not reveal such facts. It is not with me to find out holes in the personality of a person. I can at once know the holes of a person's character after seeing his palm but I keep myself reserved and do not reveal those secrets but this fellow, Kumar, enraged me and also I did not want that the gentleman should go on bearing the unfaithfulness for his future life, so I was compelled to reveal this truth.

After sometime, the atmosphere became peaceful. I was filled with a reverence for Punditji's knowledge and learning. In fact, his approach in palmistry was very deep and no fact remains secret after showing one's palm. Punditji can predict the future through the lines of the palm with the same ease as he can tell the past. In fact, our generation is proud of his personality.

Many such anecdotes were told by Anjani Nandanji to me, and so my anxiety increased. I decided that I had to reach Jodhpur anyhow and had to meet Punditji whether he meets me or not, whether he allots me time or not, I must try to see him and I believed that such a great person could not be harsh and heartless.

I firmly decided to go to Jodhpur and knew about Jodhpur from Swamiji. He told me that a train for Jodhpur is available from Delhi junction at about 8 A.M. It reaches Jodhpur the next day at about 12 noon. I also knew from him that there were several hotels and inns where people could stay comfortably. These hotels provide cheap as well as costly lodging. Dr. Shrimali's house is situated at the High Court Colony which is nearly two kilometres from the station. One can reach his home in any taxi or three-wheeler in about ten minutes.

The very next day, I got permission from Swamiji and started for my destination. I reached Jodhpur the third day. That day, I stayed in an inn opposite the Railway Station. This inn was neat and clean. From there, I rang up the phone number 22209 (now 2432209) and contacted the secretary who told me to come the next morning. On the phone, I had referred about Swami Anjani Nandanji and that it would be nice if I was allowed to come just then.

The next day at about 9 A.M. I reached his house. On the road, there stood a well-built and grand house which is the residence of Shrimaliji. From far, I found it grand, quiet and attractive.

Many persons had already collected in the lawn of the building. They had come from different parts of the country. All were showing great love and reverence for Punditji. They were there for the past three or four days and had not been given time to meet Punditji. I also took a seat and sat aside.

After sometime, Punditji himself came out and I felt greatly elated at the very first moment. I felt as if I had come out of a hot desert and found shelter under a cool place. Whatever has been written in the ancient scriptures about godly men, I found the same shape and personality—tall and well built body, the whole body moulded in a frame, broad forehead, brilliant face, sharp and cool eyes raining happiness and a fair, Aryan colour.

He was wearing ordinary but clean clothes. In his *dhoti* and shirt, he was appearing like a god-man. I bowed on his feet myself.

He asked the welfare of the persons standing there and then saw towards me. I felt that his sharp eyes had entered my heart and within a moment, it had searched the whole of my heart. Hesitatingly, I told him gently that I had heard his famous name in the field of astrology from saints and monks. Swami Anjani Nandanji, the famous saint of Northern India, had sent me to him and that I wanted some of his moments for me.

He replied that he knew my aim of coming to him and he asked me to come after two days at about 10 A.M. Then he would remove my problems. He further said that I was with Anjani Nandanji for only a week.

I knew at once that Punditji had mastered some deity, that is why he could know the purpose of my coming to him and could also know that I had been living with Swami Anjani Nandanji for only a week. When he could know all these, he would certainly be able to recognise my past and future.

At that very moment, a white woman wished him. Perhaps, she belonged to a western country and could get the opportunity to see Punditji only after a week's time. Before she spoke, Punditji said, "You are Miss Celhan, you will not get success in your object here, but you will certainly like to get answers of those questions which you have written down on a piece of paper."

Celhan's big eyes were filled with affection and surprise. She admitted that certainly she had written down some questions on a piece of paper. She wanted to ask those questions. She had folded the paper and put it in her purse. She opened her purse and took out the paper.

Punditji said, "I know what you have written. I can tell you the answers of those questions which you have written down on this piece of paper". Without seeing the paper, Punditji repeated all the four questions and he also clarified the answers to those questions.

Everyone, along with the fair-coloured lady, was surprised. How could Punditji know that there was a piece of paper containing 4 questions with Miss Celhan? Not only this, but how could Punditji tell the questions and their answers in the same order without seeing the paper?

Punditji said, "Miss Celhan, you are pregnant. The person who gave you this child will cheat you in November and will leave you for ever."

Celhan's eyes were full of tears. She started sobbing. She said that she was really perturbed by that question and the question was disturbing her peace.

Punditji said, "I knew that along with those four questions, you had one more question in your mind and you wanted a solution for it."

Celhan asked, "Will he really leave me this year by November 7?"

Punditji replied peacefully, "His heart has not changed even now and this event will happen in your life." Saying this, Punditji entered his chamber.

Celhan said that she had brought this question in her mind. How did Punditji know that I am one month pregnant and how did he know about this happening?

We were all surprised and we were also bowing with respect towards the person who had revealed the innermost matter before everybody. He had told of the past that she was pregnant and had told of the future, what would happen in November.

Third day morning, I again came to Punditji's house. There was nearly a crowd standing there but I was called in immediately. Punditji was sitting in his chamber. I wished him and sat before him on the floor.

Punditji said, "You want to engage yourself in such devotion, which is connected with making clear the future events. I assume you have a taste for the subject and have come for this very purpose."

I nodded in assent. I was filled with his knowledge, his love, his paternal affection to the brim.

I told him about my life that I knew palmistry and that I had spent nearly 30 years in learning it. I have searched every nook and corner of the Himalayas and wherever I could meet a monk or devotee who knew about palmistry, I have come in their contact and have tried to learn it.

I said, "Though I have made many new researches in palmistry and I have been working as the president of the palmistry committee for the last 6 years, but I bow before your knowledge today. I feel myself a pigmy before your knowledge. In fact, whatever knowledge I have gained in this field is negligible before your knowledge."

Punditji said with decency, "There is no limit to knowledge, I have already heard about you. I also know about the researches going on in the field of palmistry in the Himalayas. But there is much to be done in this field. If we could expand this knowledge in our life time and could contribute something to the world in this field, then our lives will go ahead towards perfection."

I stayed with Punditji for nearly a month and I have felt that he was matchless in the field of palmistry, He has done wonderful and honourable work in this field. When all of his work will be before the world, it will be a great achievement.

He has given new dimensions to palmistry and has done great research on it. Whatever new facts he has found out, are a unique contribution to the world.

In this one month, I experienced that thousands of people come to him with their problems and he meets everybody gladly, listens to their problems and provides solutions to each one of them.

One day, during conversation, he said that whichever disease comes to the body, a sign is visible on the palm. From this sign, one can know where and what sort of disease has afflicted the body and what is the solution of that particular disease.

To show an example, he said that if a white spot appears on the joint of the thumb, the person is afflicted with blood pressure. Though the scientific equipments fail to trace out the disease, yet the sign indicates that the disease has started. If this point is white, then it is the case of low blood pressure, if it is a bit reddish, it indicates high blood pressure. If one tries to find a remedy of the disease at that time, it can be removed.

In the same way, if there is a small black mark on the Health line, then it indicates a hole in the heart or heart trouble. As soon as this sign is visible, we should find the remedy.

He has evolved altogether a new method which is wonderful and revolutionary. He said that as soon as the child comes out of the womb of a mother and enters the atmosphere, the rays of the planets touch it. These rays direct the whole of his life.

To quote an example, he told that on a particular date in Jodhpur, the position of the planets and the rays emitted out by the planets, is centred on that very latitude. Those rays are helpful in the rearing up of a child and those rays direct the health of the child throughout his life.

If at that time, Mars is far away, then the rays of Mars will not influence the child so much. If at that time, the Jupiter and the Saturn are closer, then the child will be influenced more by the rays of Jupiter and the Saturn. In this way, the child receives the effect of rays of all the planets (some less and others more). A combination of all these rays directs his life.

When there is difference in cohesion of these rays, the child falls sick. For example, if at the moment of birth of the child, the Mars was yielding its effect to the tune of 27°, if out of this 27° there is plus or minus 5°, then the child suffers from the defects caused by the Mars. Now, Mars is directly related to blood circulation. So, this type of plus or minus causes diseases of blood.

He had done great work on this theory and has prepared a book consisting of nearly one thousand pages. In it, he has given details about the sickness of a person, effects of planets on the diseases and where the sign of sickness can be found on the palm.

In this way, he has searched out hundreds of signs which can be seen in the palm which can authentically determine the disease and other related things.

I got its proof after a few days. He had been invited to Delhi and was to deliver a talk on medicines and diseases before a gathering of doctors. I was accompanying him. He read his article authentically before thousands of doctors and made it clear how these signs on the palm were a boon to us. How can we know about the disease only by looking at these signs and how can we locate the diseases?

The applause which he got after delivering his lecture remains to be the most memorable moment of my life. Even the biggest physicians had started believing that perfection in Medical Science can't be attained till we accept the helping hand of palmistry.

Shrimaliji performed an experiment after delivering his speech. He called 30 such patients who were suffering from the ailment of heart. It included men, women, young and old alike. Some of them were suffering from heart and others were hale and hearty. He also asked to call those who have had heart attacks once or twice.

The chief doctor, Prof. Mathur was able to call 30 or 32 such patients, some of which were suffering from heart trouble and others were quite healthy.

Punditji stood on the dais. Every patient was brought before Punditji full covered, only the right palm uncovered. All the other parts of their bodies were not visible. One could not even judge whether they were young or old. Nothing could be known about them.

Punditji looked at every palm for hardly 5 or 7 seconds. He told his reading whether the person was still ailing from heart or had had an attack or was quite healthy.

When 30 patients had thus been examined, their charts were checked and it was found that the facts given by Punditji were authentic and tallied with their charts—cent percent.

It is a great achievement in medical science that just by looking at the palm and finding signs thereon, one can find the disease in a few seconds only, whereas the implements and examinations take two or three days to detect the disease.

Once a party came to India from Japan. They were in search of a unique personality.

It was the aim of this party to search out those personalities who were unique in their respective fields. They had read in Japan that Dr. Shrimali was unique in the field of palmistry and that he could forecast the whole of the future of a person by just seeing his palm.

This party consisted of doctors, scientists, journalists and many experienced persons who were fully mature in their fields. They believed in giving tests themselves and experimenting their own selves. They did not believe in hearsay.

When they read about Dr. Shrimali and confirmed it from the Occult Academy of Britain, they came to India only to meet Dr. Shrimali.

They had already fixed an appointment with Punditji and had informed him of their arrival. They also made clear their object of meeting him and that they were selecting such personalities of the world who were unique in their respective fields.

Fortunately, I was at Jodhpur on the day the party arrived. There were in all 18 members in this party. All of them had very sharp intelligence and logic to go to the very root of any problem.

Punditji made them sit in his drawing room and he himself sat on a sofa. I took special permission and sat on the floor of the room.

The chairman of that party said, "Punditji, we have heard your name in our country and abroad that you are an expert in the field of palmistry and that you can correctly predict the past and the future of a person."

"We are putting before you a photograph of a person's handprint. You have to tell us the maximum details about that person. We are not concerned about the future of that person but we want to know in detail about the past of that person because we know the past of that person."

He further added, "We will also not tell you that this handprint is of a man or woman. What is his age? Where does he live? We shall certainly not tell you all these things. You will have only the imprints of both his palms—only the imprints—nothing else. You have to tell us all about the person through the lines of his palms."

Punditji took both the photographs in his hands. These were the photographs of only the palms. No idea could be formed by seeing them.

Punditji looked at the photographs for a few seconds and then looked at the persons sitting opposite him. All of them were sitting like fools. They had no expressions on their faces.

Punditji started saying. "This is the hand of a person whose age at this time or at the time of taking photographs was nearly 48 years. He was born in the most ordinary family and from the sign on his palm, I find that this person lost his parents in a car accident when he was hardly one year old."

"He must have spent his life in great poverty and must have laboured very hard for his very existence. He had practically no education. At the most, he studied to the level that he was able to read only a very ordinary book. There is no sign in his hand which tells us of his proper education." Saying this Punditji glanced at the persons sitting opposite him. All the members were sitting calmly. They had no expression on their faces. One could not find from their faces whether Punditji was speaking the truth or telling lies.

Punditji added further, "When this person became 23 years old, he had his first imprisonment for committing theft. But his first term of imprisonment must have been of only 6 months. After coming out of the prison, he must have become a professional criminal."

"He must have married a widow at the age of 27 years. But that woman remained with him only for two years and then due to his habits, went away, leaving him."

"He must have gone to prison in the 32nd year of his life and this time it was a 6-year sentence. This imprisonment made him a dare-devil criminal."

"From the 38th year of his life to the 42nd year, he committed nearly six murders and in every murder, he escaped scot free because while committing murders, he did not leave any evidence and thus was saved."

"He might have again married at the age of 44 years. This marriage has given him a son and a daughter who are both alive even today."

"This man must have been 5 feet 6 inches tall, strongly built and fair-coloured. He must have been very civil in his conversations and through his talks, he would startle persons and take them in his confidence."

"But at the age of 47 years, he might have killed his wife." Saying this, Punditji raised his head and I found that all the others were sitting passively. They had neither surprise nor doubt; neither joy nor sadness on their faces. They were not expressing any feelings.

It was a serious and strict examination of Punditji because the members of the party were not expressing any sort of feelings. Punditji continued further, "This man must have cheated hundreds of persons in his life. He must have lived away from a famous city and must have collected thousands of dollars."

"The man has died just a month ago, someone has killed him and put his dead body in a well and from there people might have come to know about him."

"He must have been killed at about 1.00 P.M. on August 29th. That man is not living today," saying this Punditji put the photographs of both the palms on the table.

I saw that the members of the party remained silent for two minutes and then all the members gave a laugh of surprise and happiness. The leader of the party stood up and kissed the right hand of Dr. Shrimali and said, "You are really unique in the knowledge of palmistry. Your personality is rare and matchless. Whatever you have told through the lines on the palm is quite true and everything that you have told is authentic."

The leader of the party said, "I did not know that the lines of the palms contain so much of mystery. Truly, palmistry is a perfect and authentic science and you are unique in this field. All the information given by you has been taped and its every word is true, factual and authentic."

I took a sigh of relief. Punditji had taken a very difficult test but he had experienced hundreds of such tests and had always come out successful.

The more I came into contact with Punditji, the more deeply did I feel that he was an authority not only in palmistry but also in astrology, exorcism, occult, etc. Hundreds of monks, householders, ascetics come to him for consultations. They put their problems before Punditji and get remedies from him for all of these.

After coming into contact with Punditji, I experienced that Palmistry is, in fact, a perfect and authentic science. The future predictions done by it are true and correct. During our conversation, Punditji told me many such facts which are proving favourable in my life.

Punditji spends every moment in self-study but while talking with him, one gets such facts suddenly from him that these facts help the persons to take interest and engage themselves in such study.

Once, while talking, he said that if the Sun line moving ahead divides into two parts in the right hand, then that person will certainly get perfection and success after the 36th year of his life. In the same way, he discussed the black points found in the palm and told about their effect on a person's future. Punditji always says that one should observe the palm very minutely because every sign found on the palm is authentic in itself and shows result. So no line or point or sign should be neglected. Even the smallest sign found in the palm can clarify big possibilities.

While talking with Punditji, if only those facts are clearly understood, which he tells just by the way, then even that person may become a fully successful palmist.

When I was with him, he had perfected the idea to clarify the date of birth through palmistry. It is his firm belief that we can know the exact day, time and date of birth through palmistry. He had prepared a big thesis on it. In it, he had discussed in detail how the date of birth can be find out through palmistry.

On my question, one day he told me that it is not difficult to find out the date of birth of a person through palmistry. The lines of the palm clarify the position of planets at the time of birth. The line of Saturn can give us the year in A.D. or V.S., the line of Apollo gives the month and the lines and signs found on the mount of Mercury help in determining the date.

The thumb is very important in one's hand. This thumb determines the line of birth. Different signs on the thumb help in clarifying the time of birth.

In this way, if the lines of the palm are carefully studied, then one can determine the time and the date of birth of a person. In his thesis, he has illustrated at least the photos of a hundred persons and then clarified how to determine the time and the date of birth through the lines of the palm.

Once his class fellow came to see him. He had studied palmistry with Punditji for a considerable time and has learnt to find out the date of birth through the lines of the palm. While talking with him, he told that the lines of the palm were authentic and by means of it, the exact date of birth and the time of birth could be found out.

On inquiry from Punditji, he also corroborated the fact that the lines of the palm were quite authentic and they can help in determining the time of birth which is exact to the nearest second.

He told that even the latitude of the place of birth can also be determined by the lines of the palm. He saw the hands of three or four persons before me and clarified the time and date of birth and also their place of birth. Punditji said that after considerable practice, it does not take much time and one can know the exact time and date of birth in a few hours.

Once, out of curiosity, I asked if the horoscope could be prepared by seeing the lines of the palm. He replied that he had worked on that method quite earlier and added that horoscope could be prepared by the lines of the palm.

He said that when the time, date and place of birth are known, then with the help of a calender (*panchang*), one can prepare the horoscope within a few minutes. If one wanted to prepare a horoscope with the lines of only the right hand, then also one could do so.

He informed that the whole of our hand was divided into twelve signs of zodiac and nine planets. The necessity was to establish and understand the relationship between those signs of the zodiac and the planets. To illustrate, he said that if a particular sign of the zodiac was available on the Mount of Sun, then at the time of birth, the Sun should have been in that particular zodiac. If the sign of Cancer is found on the mount of Mercury in the palm of a person, then it is clear that Mercury was in the zodiac of Cancer when the concerned person was born.

Not only this, but there are also small lines below the signs of the zodiac which determine the degree of the zodiac. So, one can know the degree of signs of the zodiac by reading palms. Thus, by studying palms, we can prepare the horoscope and know the position of planets and their degrees clearly.

In the same way, the thumb is the most vital part of a hand. It denotes the rising of a sign of zodiac and its degrees. The sign of zodiac found on the thumb is the same sign of zodiac in which a person is born. In this way, only through thumb, the position of the planets at the time of birth of a person can be determined authentically.

Truly, this research of Punditji is revolutionary in itself. It is a challenge to the modern scientists who say that palmistry is not fully authentic. It clearly holds out that palmistry is fully authentic and factual like the other sciences.

I requested Punditji that I wanted to learn to prepare horoscope through reading, to which he agreed and it is my good fortune that he taught me this knowledge quite gladly.

The position I hold in this field and the honour I have received in this field, has at its root the knowledge given by Punditji. On the basis of this knowledge, I am considered an expert palmist in the Himalayan region. It is not every man's job to know the date of birth and prepare horoscope through the lines of the palm.

Today I feel that in reality the science of palmistry is fully authentic and through it, horoscopes can be prepared. One can also give the future prediction through it.

I have been able to take only some drops of knowledge from the ocean of knowledge of Punditji. If this little water of knowledge has been able to make my name famous in the whole of India, you can very well imagine about the ocean of knowledge which contains all sorts of knowledge.

Punditji is very calm and simple by nature. He has not even a grain of pride. He still considers himself just a student of palmistry and says that this knowledge is limitless. If we study this subject deeply, we are sure to get success.

One day, Swami Virupa Nand came to see him. Swami Virupa Nand is one of the best ascetics of the Himalayas. He stayed at Jodhpur for nearly a week. The object of his arrival was to enhance his knowledge in the field of *Mantras*. He also wanted to put his problems before Punditji.

One day, in the noon, when he was in good mood, I said to him, "I am working here with Punditji and I have learnt the method of determining the date of birth through the lines of the palm. It is my great fortune that Punditji has given me this valuable knowledge."

He revealed yet another mystery that Punditji knew this method years ago. Prior to that, he had clarified another method. It was that only through the finger of Saturn, the date of birth could be determined.

Swami Virupa Nand said, "I had learnt this method from Punditji and it is true that only through the signs found on the finger of Saturn, the date of birth can be found out."

The first phalange of the finger of Saturn tells the year of birth, the middle phalange tells the month of birth and lowest phalange tells the date of birth. Saying this, Swamiji caught hold of my hand and through the finger of Saturn, he told me my date of birth within a minute.

The next day, Swami Virupa Nand took permission from Punditji and went away. One evening, I told this fact to Punditji that he had earlier clarified the method of finding the date of birth through the finger of Saturn only. He smiled and said that one can also find the date of birth through the finger of Saturn.

In fact, Punditji has limitless knowledge of palmistry. We cannot understand that Herculean personality till we reach him. He is deep and sober like the sea.

He appears quite calm and composed but when one goes deep, one finds that his personality has limitless knowledge. It is a great good luck of our generation that he is amongst us and his guidance is available to us.

I saw many learned people coming to him in a month's time. Many ascetics, monks etc. also came to him. I also saw that householders, multimillionaires, businessmen, leaders, actors constantly come to him. In the same way, many foreigners also come to him for the solution of their problems. All of them go fully satisfied. He has neither distinction of low or high nor he is selfish. He meets everyone joyfully, listens to their problems patiently and gives solutions for them.

Once I asked him if it is necessary to master a deity to attain perfection in palmistry. He replied, "*Panchanguli* devotion is helpful in the matter." He said that for such works there were two sorts of important attainments. In the field of exorcism, it is *Karan-Pishachini* practice which is favourable for it. This practice is attained by two methods. The first method is general and favourable but it takes three months. The second is occult-based practice. It is called *Karan-Pishachini* practice by exorcism. It can be attained in only three days.

"By doing such practice, a particular female-fiend comes under control and she whispers all the past events in the ears. A person, who has attained control over the female-fiend, when sees another person or wants to know about him, then, the female-fiend tells everything before him."

"But this attainment is not fruitful in future. It is heard that Cheiro had mastered such an attainment, by virtue of which he became a world-famous palmist. But his end came deplorably. In the last days of his life, he had to struggle with hunger. So, one should abstain from such an attainment. But it is becoming very common in Western countries. Some foreigners had come to learn this and four or five of them have already learnt it and got success in it but, even then, it is my conviction that one should avoid such attainment."

"The other benevolent attainment is that of *Panchanguli*. This attainment takes nearly 21 days and when it is completed successfully, then the performer sees the past and the future of that person whose hands he touches. Whatever he sees, happens in the time to come."

"In my opinion, the attainment of Panchanguli is more useful and favourable for a performer because it is the peformance of a Goddess and it does not yield opposite influence. Besides, the performer can see the future as well as the past through this attainment."

Punditji has written a complete book on it and many performers have benefitted from it.

Punditji said that though such performances help in giving success in life and these performances give perfection to palmistry, yet it is certain that palmistry in itself is a perfect science and it does not require any performance. If we practise the knowledge correctly, we can know the past and future of a person accurately.

The more I went closer to Punditji, the greater did he appear to me. He is like an almond which looks rough and hard on the cover but if one peeps inside it, one will get fullness. I never saw him sad or frustrated. I found him full of life though he worked so hard. He utilizes every moment usefully.

I have seen him working for 20 hours a day, yet I did not find any sign of tiredness on his face. Whenever I talked with him, I found a new enthusiasm, a new hope and a new consciousness in him. I felt that he knew the value of every moment. Every moment of his life is devoted to the nation and palmistry and every moment of his life is contributed to this science.

Perhaps, our present generation may not recognize this personality correctly but the work done by this personality is significant in itself. The coming generation will be indebted to him because he has put in new researches in palmistry. These researches are solitary and the coming generation will benefit from him. There cannot be two opinions about it.

I am a mendicant. I have felt myself lonely from the very childhood, so my personality is devoid of affection but instead, I am termed as haughty, proud and critical of everything. When I came to Jodhpur, I wanted to find faults with this personality. I wanted to locate his weaknesses and remove the curtain from his incompletenesses. I have spent every minute of this one month with him but during this period, I could not find anything lacking in his personality. The more I tried to observe him, the more huge his personality appeared to me. It is the misfortune of our generation that we have not recognised this personality fully well.

If I venture to criticise him, then I should say that this man is very very simple and believes in keeping himself lonely. He has exchanges with a very few people. This is his greatness and this is his criticism. If any other person had even a grain of the knowledge which is possessed by Punditji, he would have been a very proud man. He would claim himself to be the best palmist of the world. Though Punditji has so deep and serious knowledge, yet he is engaged in research most of the time. The only aim of his life is perfection of the knowledge of palmistry and that the present and the future generation should benefit from it.

During this month, I came to know that besides the Indians, the foreigners too, were recognising his merit. They come to Punditji in the form of real students. They leave all their ego and perform such deeds which should be copied by the students. I have experienced that the foreigners get full benefit of his personality and his deep knowledge. Contrary to it, we Indians only weep for our miseries before him. We only talk about our selfish motives and do not try to make use of his knowledge.

While talking, Punditji once said, "I want to distribute my knowledge among my disciples. I want to prepare ten or fifteen such pupils who are matchless in the field of palmistry and who can influence the whole world by their knowledge. It is our great misfortune that such students are not available. They want to attain everything without labour and efforts, when it is not possible."

Still there is brightness of faith in the eyes of Punditji. He believes that some day such males and females will come in the field. They will learn the knowledge till perfection and will be able to spread it appropriately throughout the world.

I felt that Punditji practically took no rest. From 4 A.M. to 10.00 P.M., he keeps awefully busy and during this time, he makes use of every moment. He is leading the Indian Astrological Study and Research Centre. Through this centre, all the astrological, mathematical and result-oriented other jobs concerning it are authoritatively done here.

This centre is important in itself because several persons living far-away can know their future through correspondence from this centre. They can send the imprints of their hands or their horoscopes or photographs of their hands and can know about their future. Such works have been successfully completed at this centre. Very authentic and learned persons have been engaged in this centre.

In fact, it was my great fortune that I came in contact with Punditji. It was due to the fruits of my previous birth's good deeds that I could get something from Punditji.

Whatever I felt during my stay here for a month, is the wealth of my life. I saw that from morning till evening, Indian or foreign people come there. Some people came to know their future or came to get remedies of their problems. Some people came to learn exorcism, astrology or palmistry. I felt that Punditji certainly meets all of them and finds solutions to their problems.

The moment of departure was unbearable for me because I had come very close to this great personality and while staying in his house, I could get the affection of a loving mother and felt as if I was a member of the family. The love, affection and oneness which I received from this house, I could not get it in my life from anywhere. In fact, his house is like a place of pilgrimage and those people are really fortunate if they had spent some moments in this house with Punditji. I had always thought to find out some points to criticise him. Today, on objective analysis, I fail to find any such point. Maybe, people may feel it a bit exaggeration or maybe, they think that I am influenced by him and so I am saying all this but the fact is that I am famous as a proud and haughty mendicant and think myself to be a severe critic but I can say fimly and from my heart that Punditji is not only a personality but an institution in himself. Whatever he has done is the good fortune of our generation. We should be grateful to God that we living at the time when such a person is amongst us.

I feel very humble before the great knowledge of Punditji though I am the propounder of the institution. The palmistry of the Himalayan region and my post is held very high. But I don't consider myself more than a feeble lamp before the knowledge of Punditji. It was after my humble request that he allowed me to write a few words about him in this book. It is due to his greatness, I feel very proud after writing these few words because I got an opportunity to express my innermost feelings in this book.

—YOGI CHAITANYA

INTRODUCTION

God has so made human life, especially the construction of a man's body, that inspite of the very best efforts of all the scientists of the world to know about his intricate structure, they are not getting success in their aims. The more they try to solve this mystery, the more they get entangled. The aim of all knowledge and science in this world is to understand the human being, his behaviour and to keep him happy but this is possible only when one is able to know the latent secrets of a man beforehand because these secrets spoil the whole thing by appearing suddenly in the form of uncertainties. *'Future'* is such a word which is in itself a secret, very tedious and inaccessible in its meaning. All branches of science are trying to understand and know about the future happenings but they have not succeeded in their objective so far. If there is anything which can throw light on this 'mystery' or help in understanding this, it is only the **science of palmistry** which most learned men have accepted with one voice.

Man has always been endeavouring to know the future. He is always apprehensive of the unknown future. He thinks whether the work he is doing at present and on which he is staking all the labour, wisdom and money of his life, may not be fruitful in the time to come and he remains apprehensive all the time thinking this.

Sometimes I wonder about God and bow my head before his greatness with honour. How efficient an artist he is that he has depicted the future incidents or happenings by means of zig-zag lines on a human palm. I also hold our ancient holy sages in high esteem who have solved the mystery of these lines with their divine insight and penance and made this knowledge easy for the coming generations.

It is necessary to take into consideration several factors while studying the lines on a palm. The very first thing is not to base one's reading by looking at one line only because just one line cannot reveal the truth about the individual but other lines complimentary to it are also helpful in showing the truth. Just as there are hundreds of small and big parts in a railway engine and each part has its own importance in its place, and if any of the parts gets out of order, the whole engine will stop working; similar is the case of lines on a palm. If the assisting lines are not studied carefully along with the main lines, or the importance of these assisting lines is more or less ignored, there is possibility of a serious mistake in arriving at the correct conclusion. Therefore, it is necessary for an expert palmist not to pass over any line found on the palm. On the other hand, he should give equal importance to the smallest lines as to the big and prominent lines.

The lines made by God on a man's hand were made after very careful thought. Each line found on the palm has its own importance and is closely connected with some other line. If we give our reading by looking at only one line, there is a likelihood of mistake. Therefore, the main lines and its helping lines should be studied carefully simultaneously and then only the future be told. Some persons are desirous of knowing whether importance be given to the right hand or the left hand. Different people have different views in this connection. Some people give importance only to the right hand. For them the left hand is unimportant while others give importance only to the left hand. They think that the right hand, being in active use, lines on it get altered very quickly while lines on the left hand remain constant for a much longer period. Some people are of the opinion that both the hands should be studied side by side but I think all these schools of thought are incomplete in a sense. The views formed by these learned men are based on popular beliefs or on their little knowledge. In fact, an authentic description is found in the book, *'Hasta Rekha Sanjiwani'* in this connection.

Palmistry specialists should give special emphasis on the right hand because we do most of the work in our lives with the right hand; hence our activity can only be judged from the right hand. Here one should keep it in mind that if a person uses his left hand for writing purposes or if he performs most of the activities by his left hand, then his left hand should be given importance. In the same way, the right hand of such women should be studied who are earning their own livelihood and are actively engaged in earning money by their intelligence or efforts.

A question arises here that if the right hand has all the importance in life, then what is the use of the left hand? I have already made this point clear that the left hand be given due importance if a person writes or works with the left hand or if this hand is more active. Along with this, the left hand of those females should be studied who are dependent upon others; their husbands or fathers. Similarly, the left hand of those persons who are unemployed or are incapable of earning, be given due importance while giving future reading. At the same time, it should be kept in mind that the help of the left hand should be taken while giving importance to the right hand of a man, if something is not clear in the right hand. Like this, if some fact or happening is found in both hands, it should be accepted as authentic.

Similarly, if a woman is in government service or engaged in independent business, her right hand should be seen but if something is not very clear, then it should be made clear by studying her left hand.

A question arises: whether future-reading can be correctly and successfully made clear by studying the lines on a palm? Some people have doubts in this. Quite a number of persons expressed this view before me: "How can the future results be predicted by looking at the lines on a palm which go on changing frequently? Some persons also questioned that according to learned men all the lines on a hand get completely changed in 7 years' time, then prediction of 10 or 20 years ahead is, therefore, almost impossible.

But just as I have already explained, these ideas have been propagated by those persons who did not have a deep knowledge of palmistry or whose knowledge is confined to books only. The fact is that the lines on a hand do not change, the main lines on a hand remain as they are. Their helping lines appear for sometime and after giving some hints for future happenings, disappear. Along with this, there are surely some signs on a hand which are formed for sometime and then disappear. The formation of these signs is an indication of some special happenings. Similarly, the disappearance of these also is in itself an indication of some special happening. Therefore, these signs by their formation and disappearance give indication of the future happenings.

Along with this, it is also clear that these signs may disappear but they leave the mark of their having been there and such marks remain there permanently. To say, therefore, that some signs disappear permanently is not true. A palmist is able to draw conclusions about future happenings by means of these signs and the effect they leave on a palm.

I have experimented to gain the experience for proving the authenticity of palmistry. You will be surprised to know that there are special signs for special facts and the individuality of a person can be understood by means of those special signs. Just as to understand a horoscope and to predict correctly the future with its help, the astrologer takes into consideration the main *'graha'* (planet) which affects the whole individuality of the person. When the importance of that particular *'graha'* is realized and understood, the whole picture of the person is clear before our mind. Similarly, it is necessary to know about the most prominent signs on a palm by means of which complete individuality of the man can be visualized. I have seen the palms of approximately 4,000 murderers (who had committed the heinous crime with their own hands) for experimentation and discovered that all had one common sign on their hands, that the murderer's thumb was small and the tip of the thumb was flat, also that the nail of the thumb was small and more or less round in shape. This sign is a special sign of its kind and this fact has been made clear by means of this experiment that if the thumb of a person is smaller in proportion to his fingers and thicker and the top of the thumb is thickly built, at the same time the nail on it is round, the man certainly must have been a murderer in his life and will lead a prison term for committing some murder.

Once a connected happening made this clear. One day an unknown mill-worker came to me and opened his palm before me in order to know his future. In his full hand, the thumb seemed to be more or less separate from the hand and I was able to locate all the above mentioned signs of a murderer on his hand. Immediately this came to my mind that this person should be a murderer and his hand should have been blood-stained.

Now the question arises: at what age will he commit the murder? What will be its time? To know it one needs to consider the mount of Saturn and the line of Saturn. The point where the line of Saturn breaks, if a straight line is drawn from that point towards the lifeline, the point, at which this line will meet the lifeline, is the indicating point. Now, according to this point, or the distance between this point and lifeline, will indicate the age of the person at which he may commit this kind of a heinous crime. This fact can be known only by experience.

When the workman opened his palm before me, his age at that time was about 45 years and from this point when I calculated, I found that this work (murder) must have been done when he was of about 40 years of age. I stared at him for a few moments and told him that he might try to save himself or try to throw dust in the eyes of the law, but he would not escape the law. He would have to go to jail soon because he had murdered someone in his lifetime.

He looked strangely at me. He must have thought in his heart how could this man know the fact while till that day, he had been fooling the police and was escaping the clutches of law. Without wasting a moment, he immediately withdrew his hand and went out of my room like an arrow. His going out in this way was the proof of what 1 had told. I have not seen him till date. We have this fact for the last many years. I had the privilege of going through a handwritten book of the 12th century in which it was clearly stated that a man, having a small flat thumb with a nail almost circular in shape accompanied with a cross or sign on the mount of Mars, must be a murderer.

He had written this as a result of his own experience and his experience continued to be confirmed in future generations. He made further experiments in this connection and came to the conclusion that really a man with these signs on his hand actually happens to be a murderer.

After this, another book entitled *"Hastarekhayen"* was published in the 19th century. This fact was mentioned in this book also and this knowledge reached me passing from generation to generation and this knowledge will go on benefiting for generations to come and will go on developing. But this even has clearly proved that the indication of lines on a hand give correct reading and they tell the bare naked truth and nothing else. Whatever mystery is hidden in them, is fully authentic. The need is for a person who can understand this secret and read the lines properly.

I want to give one more example to prove that whatever facts the lines reveal, these are bare facts and absolute truth in themselves. The approach of death or the hour of death is clearly indicated by lines of the palm well in advance. Six months before the day of death, a net of zig-zag lines is formed on the nail of the finger of Saturn. When this net is visible, it should be assumed that the man will not survive for more than six months. In my lifetime, I have seen the hands of about 16-20 persons who were perfectly healthy when 1 saw these signs on their hand but I received the news of their death within 5 or 6 months. Exactly in the same way, there are three kinds of lines in connection with death:

1. If the lifeline comes to an abrupt stop and at the spot where it stops, a black-mark or cross-sign is found and if a line is drawn from this cross towards the lifeline, the resultant time will be the age of the person.
2. If the heartline has disappeared on the way and may be suddenly visible under the mount of Saturn, then it should be understood that the man will die prematurely and will not be able to enjoy full age.
3. If the heartline meets the headline under the mount of Saturn or the Mount of Jupiter and similar combination is visible on the other hand also, then the man will not live his full age. My meaning of full age is the average age of the people in a particular country. In India, the full age is considered to be between 60 and 70 years. If a man dies at the age of 40 to 50 years, such a death is considered premature.

These facts are indicative of incomplete age. If such a sign is seen, it becomes clear first of all that the man's age will be incomplete and what would be his correct age can be found by drawing a line from this sign to the 'lifeline' or by estimating one can ascertain the correctness of his age when he would die.

In the above lines, I was trying to make it clear that palmistry is not to be laughed at or there is no need to disbelieve it but instead, these lines are a help to prove the fact. At the same time, no other science can make the future reading as clear as these lines do.

Several things should be taken into consideration while studying Palmistry and some of those facts are as given below:

1. Don't touch the hand of any person who comes to show you his hand because the electric current of your body will come in contact with the current in his body and the genuine

features of his hand will be finished. Therefore, keep your hands folded while seeing any hand.
2. At first, the back of both the hands of the man should be seen as in this position, that is, by keeping the palm facing the ground, you will be able to understand the shape of his hand clearly as to whether the hand is circular, square or what kind of hand has been placed before you.
3. On knowing this fact, ask the man to turn his hands and after both the hands are in correct position, palms facing the sky, then start seeing from the wrist and thus go ahead.
4. After this, the mounts, their protrusion, fingers joined to the mounts and the thumb should be seen. At the end, the forepart of the fingers and the nail be seen.
5. In this way, the study of the hand should be done without touching it and the joints of the whole hand should be taken into consideration. The study of the planets can be completely done by looking at the joints of the palm on the hand. Several facts are revealed by looking at the joints of the fingers. The touch of the hand will give you an indication whether the hand is soft or hard, flexible or stiff. The softness and hardness of the hand is also of great importance in the study of palm.
6. The bracelets also bear importance for a palmist and these should also be studied.
7. After this, the mounts on the palm, protrusions of the mounts or their depression, also the lines joining the mounts, the merger of two mounts and even the minute signs found there should also be taken into consideration.
8. At the end, the circles and horns, which are formed at the end of the fingers and which also have their own importance, should be studied.

THE METHOD OF SEEING A HAND

1. Ordinarily, a hand can be seen at anytime but the best time for this is morning time when the person wishing to show his hand has neither had breakfast nor taken food. It is my experience that the blood circulation gets speedier after taking food due to which the minor lines on the hand become

almost invisible. Under such conditions, a magnifying glass should be used invariably.

2. A person showing his hand or the questioner should have taken bath before showing the hand. Getting up just after sleep, dirty or lazy body, makes the atmosphere unbecoming and it causes hindrance in foretelling.
3. One should neither show a hand after heavy meals or after strenuous exercise nor should it be shown after working continuously as this is not favourable.
4. A hand should not be shown when it is very hot or cold weather as when it is very hot, the palm becomes rather red and it is not possible to find out its natural colour.
5. No person after taking drinks or intoxicants or in sub-normal condition should go to the palmist.

Just as there are some rules for the person showing a hand, similarly, the observance of some rules are necessary for the palmist also.

1. The palmist should not see the hand while he is in an angry mood or is in a perturbed state for any other reason. A polite 'no' should be said to a person who by chance comes to show his hand at that time.
2. The prophesying of 'good or bad' regarding a person should not be explained in the very beginning, soon after seeing a hand. This can create many problems. For example, if there is an indication of death after a month, it is not good to let him know this even in a roundabout way.
3. A hand should be examined in an unconcerned manner. The palmist cannot remain unconcerned if the person is a loved one or hostile to him, otherwise future telling becomes more or less unrealistic.
4. The result of the reading should be told after full satisfaction by reading the hand and verification with the other hand.
5. A palmist can foretell the future with certainty after studying the hand, taking into consideration the above-mentioned facts. Just as a person can see his image in clean mirror, similarly, the palmist can read the future by studying the hand.

◆◆

Hand : A Study

The wrist is a part which acts as a link in joining the hand to the arm. The fore-part of the wrist is called the 'palm' and the signs found on the palm are very important for a palmist.

The palm is composed of small bones. There are nearly 14 bones joined together, which give a shape to the palm. In the front part of these bones, there are 3 more pieces of bones composing each finger and 2 more composing each thumb. The upper ends of the bones are protected with nails.

From the wrist up to the end of the finger of Saturn is termed as 'hand'. According to the science of palmistry, there are five kinds of hands:

1. Very small hand
2. Small hand
3. Ordinary hand
4. Long hand
5. Very long hand

I have already made it clear that to see the formation of the hand, it should be reversed 'palm facing towards the ground'. The kind of the hand can be easily known if the hand is placed in this position. Much can be known about the person by the study of the kind of hand the person has.

1. Very Small Hand: Persons of this kind are narrow-minded and suspicious by nature. They go on quarrelling for their small gains. They give top priority to their own selfish aims and if truth is to be told, cheating, cunningness and opportunism is part of their personality. It is in their nature to talk ill of others, to bring them down in the eyes of others and to act in an unfriendly manner towards others. In the eyes of the society or the country, such persons have no value and do not contribute anything.

2. Small Hand: In a way, such persons can be called lazy. Though these people have high dreams and are ready to do much on the basis of their imagination but too much idleness is present in their lives, as a result of which they can never put to practical use their plans. They like boosting themselves, exaggeration and creation of false atmosphere around them. They act in such a manner that this illusory and suspicious environment prevails around them. It is true that they have sharp brains but they do not know how to make use of opportunities and repent when the time has passed. Such persons, though able and competent, don't fully succeed in their lives.

3. Ordinary Hand: Such persons are full of practical wisdom. They know very well what, when and how to talk with one and how to behave with a person. They have all these points in their mind and so they are said to possess practical wisdom while dealing with other persons.

They get due respect in society and give proper thought and time to everything before doing it. They constantly face struggle in their lives and they are able to achieve success in life on the basis of these struggles and manage to gather facilities. Ordinarily, their health remains good. The greatest thing found in them is that they have the capacity to mould themselves according to the conditions prevalent.

4. Long Hand: Such persons are generally useful to the society. They have a trait in their personality that they are neither very happy nor are full of anxiety. They are very practical in their dealings with others, are clever and promising. They are able to reach quickly at the bottom of any problem placed before them and their finding in connection with the thing or its results generally are found to be fully correct in the end. The opinion formed about any unknown person, his character, his efficiency and the way of his working, all these turn out to be fully correct in future. Such persons are said to be more useful to the society.

5. Very Long Hand: Such persons are not of any special use to the society. They are too emotional and live in an imaginary world. They get perturbed when they have to face struggles and when they are placed in such situations. They are not competent or strong enough to challenge such situations.

Some other facts should also be known along with the kind of hand. The hand can be broad or narrow, can be hard or soft. In the same way, when we take somebody's hand in our hand, then it may be dry or moist. It is necessary for a palmist to understand all these facts. It should also be understood whether the shape of the tips of fingers are pointed or circular or flat. The knots between the one and the other phalange should also be studied. These knots can be thick or thin. In the same way, the length of each knot has its own importance. It has been proved by experience that a person turns out to be very wise, learned and famous if the upper portion of the little finger protrudes beyond the third phalange of the finger of Apollo and such person is likely to attain some high position in life. It has been found that the persons whose little finger is found to be long, succeed well in their lives. The object of what I say is that we should take into consideration the length of the fingers also while studying a hand.

NAMES OF FINGERS

There are 4 fingers and 1 thumb in every man's hand. The thumb is also called *'angustha'* and it has 2 phalanges.

1. Index Finger (Tarjani): This finger is next to the thumb and is called the Index finger *(tarjani)*. It has three phalanges. While studying this finger, it should be taken into consideration as to what kind the tip of the finger is and to which direction is leaning. The leaning is of three kinds. Some fingers are absolutely straight while others are leaning towards the thumb. Similarly, some fingers may be leaning towards the finger of Saturn.

2. The Finger of Saturn: This is the longest finger on the hand and is called *'Madhyama'* in Sanskrit. It should be borne in mind while studying this finger whether the knots between the phalanges are very much prominent or are ordinary. There are very few hands on which the index finger and the finger of Saturn are of equal length. In case, the index finger and the finger of Saturn are equal, the person either commits suicide or dies through an unnatural cause.

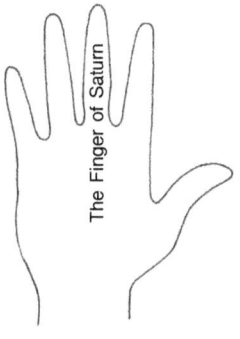

3. The Finger of Apollo: The finger adjoining the finger of Saturn is called the finger of Apollo. Ordinarily, this finger is smaller than the finger of Saturn and is almost equal to the index finger in length. The leaning of this finger should be carefully studied. If it is leaning towards the finger of Saturn, then it is considered excellent. Its leaning towards the opposite side indicates that the person's family life cannot remain much happy.

4. The Little Finger or the Finger of Mercury: It is the smallest finger on the hand. Ordinarily, its end reaches the tip of the finger of Appollo or reaches up to the upper joint. If the finger is unusually long on the hand of any person, he will aussuredly be very fortunate and will reach a very high position with his own efforts.

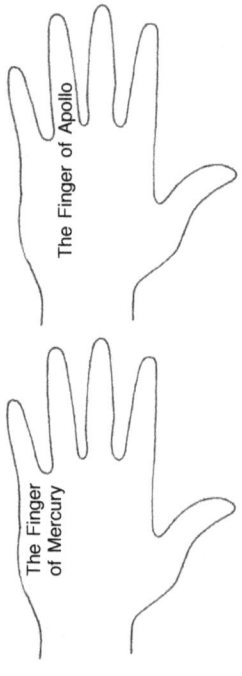

FORMATION OF HAND

The kind of hand depends upon the heaviness or thinness of the bones of the palm. We can divide the hand into 7 kinds on the below mentioned criteria:

1. Primary Hand.
2. Square Hand.
3. Workman's Hand.
4. Philosopher's Hand.
5. Artist's Hand.
6. Ideal Hand.
7. Mixed Hand.

I am explaining the different specialities of these kinds of hand in the following lines:

1. The Primary Hand: This kind is commonly coarse, heavy and fatty. The formation of this hand is asymmetrical and ugly and its fingers appear to be asymmetrical. In fact, such persons cannot be termed as fully civilized. They have a special tendency to copy things. They are civilized, but do not have the characteristic cultural ingredients. In a way, such persons are completely materialistic. The main aim of their lives are food, clothes and a house to live in. They do not understand the values of life other than these.

Though it is true that such persons are laborious and whatever they earn in their lives. is dependent upon their labour. They get annoyed on very trivial things in their lives. Breaking of law is a very easy task for them. From socialistic and ethical points of view, such persons come under the category of criminals.

2. Square Hand: If we see the reverse side of the hand, this kind of hand can be easily recognised. There are several knots on this kind of hand. Asymmetrical hands with prominent bones come under this class. There is, however, difference between the primary hand and this hand that the fingers of this kind of hand have a special kind of suppleness by which the hand can be easily recognised. Such hands are thinner and less coarse in comparison to the Primary Hand.

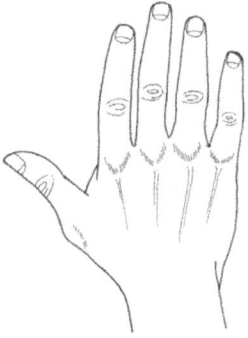

Square Hand

Such persons are genius and intellectuals. The community always receives contributions from them. Only such persons are capable of leading the society and leave some special inheritance for the future generation. Persons with such hands are philosophers, artists, painters, men of letters, psychologists, etc. Though it is true that such persons are not affluent but they do not attach so much importance to money in their lives as to their reputation, respectability and fame.

3. Workman's Hand: This kind of hand is a little more lengthy in proportion to its width. The beginning of the hand is bit fathy and the front part is a bit lighter in its comparison. The mounts found on the palm are muscular and hard and most of the mounts are suppressed and heavy. Such persons remain active in their lives and go on doing one or the other kind of work. They don't like to sit idle. They make their position secure and favourable and gain

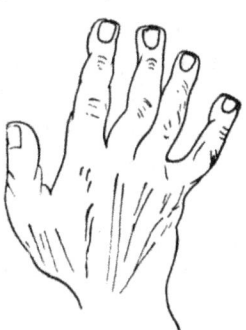

Workman's Hand

complete success in life by their own efforts even though they are born in an ordinary class of society. They achieve complete success in their lives. In their work, there is a great harmony of thought, sentiments and energy.

4. Philosopher's Hand: Such persons do not work on sentiments but they keep harmony between sentiments and practicability. To initiate new works, to open new vistas and to do new things is their nature. Successful personality is their main characteristic.

Persons with such hands are learned and intellectuals. They are more useful to the society and have proved to be natural leaders. They do such deeds which enhance the society and glorify the country.

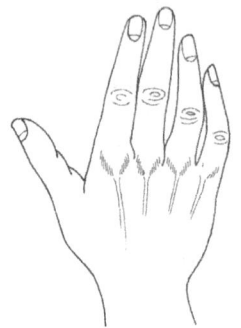

Philospher's Hand

Such persons have full faith in ideals and beliefs. They always remain desirous in intellectual pursuits and ever ready for increasing their knowledge and intelligence and can be found to be doing good-turn to people. Great philosophers, thinkers and intellectuals are bestowed with such hands. They are deficient of wealth in their lives, even then, they are highly respected.

5. Artist's Hand: This kind of hand is soft, supple and tender. It has a pink tinge and is very beautiful to look at. The joints of all bones are of equal proportion and such hands can be easily recognised with the help of their fingers. Their fingers are thin, long, artistic and well formed.

Such persons are by nature lovers of art and beauty. A kind of desire is always present in their hearts for art and they constantly think of art. They themselves are artists and see other

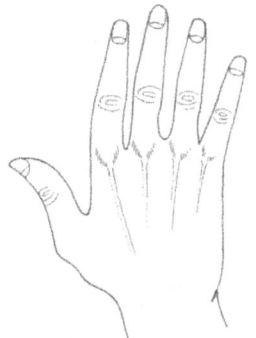

Artist's Hand

persons also in the same manner. They are true connoisseurs of art, and if for some reason they themselves cannot become artists, a greater portion of their wealth is spent in artistic pursuits.

Such persons have a special bent for love but they generally remain love-torn. From the worldly point of view, these persons are not successful as they remain engrossed in emotions and imaginations. Financial anxiety is all the time present in their lives and they are lazy by nature.

I have concluded by experience that if an artist's hand is not so supple but a little inclined towards stiffness, then such persons can amass wealth by means of arts and also succeed in earning fame.

6. Ideal Hand: In fact, this is said to be the best kind of hand. This kind of hand is commonly well-formed, soft, accompanied with a special kind of suppleness. Such hand is neither much long nor much wide.

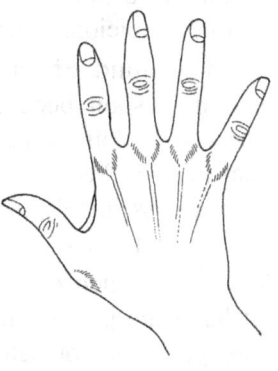

Ideal Hand

Such persons come to know future happenings in advance, that is, they can do foreboding in their lives and believe in reaching the very root of the problem. They have to face too many obstacles and struggles in their lives; but they do not budge by seeing these difficulties. On the other hand, they go on moving forward on their path constantly. They do not lose hope in life even though several times they are insulted and are ignored by the society.

From worldy point of view, such persons live only on ideals. As a result of this, the social life of such persons generally remains unsuccessful. Even then, they are firm in their determination and they only leave a work after thoroughly completing it, once they take it up in their hands. Their contribution to the society in this way is a form of a boon.

Idealists and dreamers are mostly found to be unfit in worldly affairs, still they believe in living with kingly grandeur and style without possessing riches and do not hesitate to starve if the money gets exhausted. The end of their lives is very troublesome and full of woes and miseries.

7. Mixed Hand: This is said to be the last kind of hand. The hand which cannot be included in any of the six above-mentioned categories, can be included in this kind. In this kind of hand, good points of more than one kind of hand are discovered; hence it can be called 'Mixed Hand'. For example, the shape of the mixed hand is a combination of a philosopher and a workman's hand.

This mixure of characteristics of hands can be seen in their character and behaviour as well. Such persons begin a work in such haste that their anxiety for hasty completion gradually gets worn out and they leave the work incomplete, beginning a new one. Their mind is constantly full of suspicion, apprehension and uncertainty.

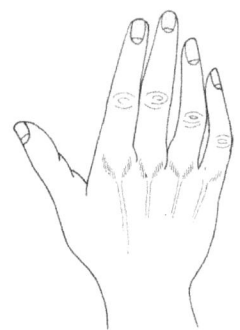

Mixed Hand

The mind of such a person is uncertain and they soon become hopeless if they don't succeed in doing a particular work and, for this reason, they become self-centred. Such persons get success in life after many efforts.

Thus, I have made clear the seven kinds of hands in the above lines. It is much necessary for a palmist to first of all study the kind of hand the person sitting in front of him is showing and to know the specialities or deficiencies therein. Keeping in view the kind of hand, if he studies the other lines found in the hand, he will be very near to the complete success of a correct reading of the palm and his future reading in one way will be based scientifically.

Hand-Palm, Fingers and The Foreparts of Fingers

Fingers and the formation of a hand has special significance in the study of a hand. A big hand by itself is called a significant hand. Such persons are sharp-sighted and are experts in their dealings. Contrary to this, persons with small hands are short-tempered, crazy and of unsteady nature. Such persons cannot get full success in life.

Here and in the following pages, wherever a hand is mentioned, it means the palm.

PALM

From the base of fingers upto the first ring of the bracelets is known as 'the length of the palm' and from the base of the thumb upto the other end is known as 'the breadth of the palm'. All the signs on this whole part of the palm are very important for a palmist.

1. Narrow Palm: Such persons are generally of weak temperament. They only give importance to their own selfish ends and they don't care if the other person gets harmed in this act of theirs. To lay trust on such persons cannot be said to be a very wise thing.

2. Wide Palm: Persons with wide palms are of determined nature and are strong-hearted. There is no difference in their preaching and practice and they stick to what they once say. If they give some kind of assurance to anybody, they try to fulfil it as far as possible.

3. Very Wide Palm: Such persons generally are of unstable nature. Their palms are more wide than long in this case. Such persons are not able to take quick decisions and do a lot of thinking before doing anything.

There is no orderliness of doing anything in their lives. They take in their hands more than one work at the same time and none can be completed properly, due to which disappointment gets deeprooted in their minds. Generally, such persons remain unsuccessful in life.

4. Palm With Equal Dimensions: Persons, whose palms are of equal dimensions, that is, the length and breadth are equal, are healthy, strong, quiet and strong-willed. Such persons are called fully energetic. All they turn out to be or whatever progress they make in their lives, is all due to their own efforts.

They are determined. They don't take up any work in hand unless they are convinced of its success. Once they start doing a thing, they put in all their energy and heart for its success and do not rest till it is fully and properly completed. This is the secret of their success in life.

KIND OF PALM

Much importance is attached to the kind of hand in future-reading. The palmist should see the kind of hand it is as soon as he touches a hand. I am explaining it clearly below:

1. Tender Hand: Persons with such hands are generally imaginative. There is a special kind of adaptability and tenderness in their nature and their lives are shaped likewise. They are prepared to help other persons at anytime. Mostly ladies have such hands. If one feels such a hand in case of a male, it can be understood that lady-like traits are prominent in that male.

2. Loose and Tender Hand: Persons with soft and rather loose hands are generally useless, lazy and very selfish. They do not know what kindness means. Hands of culprits are mostly like this. Such persons are always leaders of anti-social and evil works. Such persons are heartless, cheats and perpetrators of deceitful acts.

3. Stiff Hand: The life of such persons is dry and they are hard-hearted. They remain stiff and uncompromising even in matters of love and treat love matters as a matter of war. If the hand is very hard, they are simple labourers. Such persons give greatest importance to their own work. They do not get frustrated even when faced with problems; on the contrary, they continue to do their work constantly.

Age of a person should also be taken into consideration while studying a hand. Commonly, a hand is less stiff in young age but it becomes stiffer in advanced age. My object in saying this is that the age should be taken into consideration while deciding the kind of hand. Generally, people with stiff hands are not intellectuals but they earn their livelihood by sheer manual labour.

4. Very Stiff Hand: Persons with such a hand depict lack of intelligence and sense of tyranny. They feel happy by seeing other men in trouble and remain perfectly selfish. The hands of culprits are like this. Such signs can be seen on the hands of executioners or professional murderers.

The colour of hand should also be seen side by side with the kind of hand. But care should be taken to find out the natural colour of the hand before touching the palm. The colour of the hand gets changed when the palm is touched and it does not retain its original colour.

1. Red: A man with red colour hand is short-tempered and is of suspicious nature. Such persons are of very touchy temperament and no one can find out as to when he will get angry. Generally, such a person is narrow-minded and imprudent.

2. Too Much Red: A man with very red hand is cruel, with criminal tendencies and is more than enough selfish. He does not hesitate to cheat his friends if a chance comes. He is so selfish that he will not lose the chance of taking advantage of an opportunity if he gains only one paisa while the other loses full 100 rupees. Such men will surely cheat though they are treated kindly. To repose trust in such persons is not free from danger.

3. Pink: A man with pink (light rosy) colour is healthy, kind hearted and has high ideals. A nobility is seen in the mode of his living. Such persons succeed in their lives with their own efforts and work and succeed in reaching a very high position from a modest beginning. In fact, only such persons can contribute something to the society.

4. Yellow (Pale): Pale colour is indicative of sickness. If a person's palm appears to be pale, it can be concluded that he is sick or there is something wrong in his blood. Such a person is of unstable and irritable nature. At the same time, he is weak-minded because of feeble intelligence.

5. Smooth Skin: The skin of the hand also has its own importance. A person with soft and smooth skin is kind-hearted, sympathetic and constantly moves towards his goal. He has a clear aim and goes on moving forward continuously. It is this kind of man who generally succeeds in life.

6. Dry Skin: Persons, whose palm-skin is dry, are generally sick and of unstable nature. They are unable to take any decision independently but they follow and act on the advice of others. There is no co-ordination in their work. They are nearly sick both mentally and physically. They can get success in life after great efforts.

7. Coarse Skin: Too much dry and coarse skin is indicative of weakness and diseased lover. Such persons are of suspicious nature and having weak mentality, generally remain unsuccessful in life.

NAILS

The nails on the fingers should also be taken into consideration while studying a palm. Ordinarily, these nails are at the tip of the fingers and help in protecting the fingers.

There are two functions of nails from the scientific point of view:

(i) To protect the tips of fingers so that the fingers do not get damaged or hurt by a blow from outside and these nails help in enhancing the beauty of the fingers.

(ii) These are good conductors of electricity. The natural electricity present in the atmosphere enters the body through these nails. Not only this, but the rays of other planets also enter through these nails and help in making the individual work smoothly.

1. Short Nails: Short nails reveal that the man is uncivilized. If a man has short nails on his finger, it should be understood at once that though he might have been born in a high family, yet, by nature, he is narrow-minded, weak and of wicked tendencies.

2. Short and Pale Nails: Such nails reveal wickedness of the individual. These nails also indicate that the person tells lies at every step and will deceive his own family members at the time of need. Such a person can never be trustworthy.

3. Short and Rectangular Nails: A person having such nails on his fingers is a heart patient and dies of heart attack.

4. Short and Wide Nails: Such persons believe in quarrelling. Criticising and interfering in others' works is their favourite pastime and are of stubborn nature.

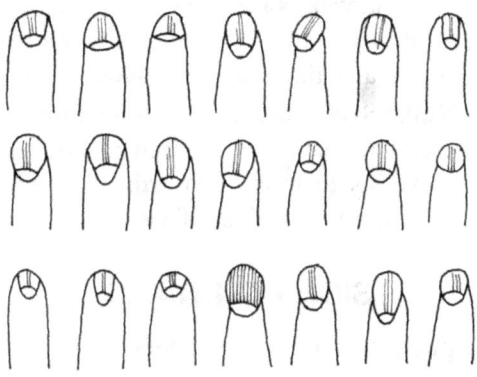

Different Types of Nails

5. Hard and Narrow Nails: Generally, such persons are of quarrelsome nature. Once they make up their minds, they will surely do it whether it be right or wrong but they don't care for it. On the other hand, they stick to their decision and it is not good to trust such persons.

6. Square Nails: Square nails reveal the weakness of persons. Such nails show that the man is coward, timid and subdued.

7. Short and Triangular Nails: Such nails are generally wide at the upper tip and narrow at the lower end. Persons with such nails are lazy and shirk to work. Such persons find themselves cut-off from the society and feel lonely.

8. Nails Wider in Proportion to Length: Such persons become easily angry but are firm about their work and complete the work once they take it up in their hands. They don't like undue interference from anyone in their works. In a way, they like loneliness.

9. Short Nails and Knotty Fingers: Such persons are of quarrelsome type. If such nails are found on the fingers of a female, it means that she must be completely overpowering her husband and must be of quarrelsome nature.

10. Rounded Nails: Persons having rounded nails at the tips are firm-minded and take quick decisions. Such persons know how to act on the decision so taken.

11. Thin and Long Nails: Persons with thin and long nails are weak in body and are fickle-minded. They cannot take independent decisions but act on the advice given by others.

12. Long and Curved Nails: Such persons are not of good character and they do have affairs with others than their own wives. They get bad name many times in their lives.

13. Perfect Nails: Such nails are little longer than wider and have their natural lustre. They are men of high ideals, good-intentioned and are always desirous to move forward. Only such persons can be called successful from all points of view.

SIGNS ON NAILS

1. Black Spots: It should be understood that a man having black spots on his nails is destined to meet with great calamity and misfortune. It should be known that spots appear on nails for sometime while at other times, these disappear also. Black spots on nails are an indication of impurity of blood. One is soon to get sick with small-pox, malaria, fever or any such disease connected with the impurity of blood.

2. White Spots: White spots on nails indicate obstructions in the circulation of blood and they are indicative of future disease. If such spots appear on the nails of the finger, it should be concluded that the man is likely to be sick very soon.

3. Nails with Half Moon at their Base: Half moon appears at times at the base of nails. They are indicative of progress as follows:

(i) Half moon on the index finger indicates promotion in service or some good news is likely to be heard.

(ii) Half moon on the finger of Saturn is indicative of the fact that the person is likely to get benefit from machinery and there is possibility of his getting money or some good news unexpectedly.

(iii) Half moon on the finger of Apollo indicates that the persons will soon get rise in status and respect in society.

(iv) The half moon formed on the little finger indicates the likelihood of profit in business dealings.

(v) The half moon appearing at the base of the thumb indicates all kinds of auspiciousness, progress and is indicative of some good news.

4. Nails with Big Half Moon: I have described the short half moon above, but several times a big half moon which covers almost half the nail is visible. If big half moon is visible, it shows contrary results. The result would be contrary to the results of every finger given above.

I have given description of black and white spots above. It would be proper to know that a white spot on the thumb is indicative of love while the back spot shows committing of crime in the near future. Likewise, a black spot on the index finger reveals loss; contrary to this, white spot is indicative of profit in business. If a white spot is visible on the nail of the finger of Saturn, it is indicative of journey to be undertaken soon, while the black spot is sign of the death of some old person in the family. Similarly, a black spot on the nail of the finger of Apollo soon results in getting defamation in society. On the other hand, if a white spot is seen on the nail of this finger, then the man will soon get respect, money and fame. White spots on the finger of Mercury is indicative of success in achieving one's aim while the black spot shows failure in achieving it.

If yellow spots are visible on one or more fingers, it is certain that the man will meet his death in the near future.

At times, tiny red spots are also visible. According to astrology, these also are indicative of bad omens and if red spots are seen on one or more fingers of a man, it shows that the man may soon be murdered.

In fact, nails and signs found on the nails have much importance in themselves. Therefore, while studying a hand, the palmist should also keep in mind all these factors.

KNOTS

Fingers cannot be formed without knots but these are very prominent in the hands of some persons. In fact, the prominent parts are named as 'knots'. What I mean by knots is that there is a joint at conjuction of every phalange which is clearly visible, but in soft fingers, these knots can neither be felt nor be seen.

Every finger has three parts which are formed with the help of two joints. In some persons, only one knot is seen while the other may not be seen. In others, both knots can be seen clearly, while in a few others, even one knot is not visible.

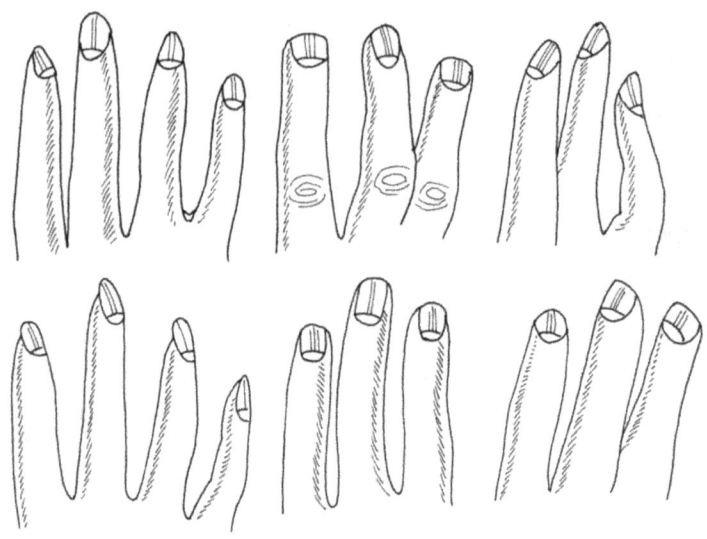

Different Types of Foreparts of Fingers

Ordinarily, these knots are indicative of thoughts, work and inspiration. I am giving below some facts in this connection:

1. If only the lower knot in the index finger is felt, then such persons are of low intellect, but if only the upper knot is felt, then they are clever and efficient in their work. If both the knots are visible in the index finger, then such persons remain idle and inactive in life. On the other hand, if there is not a single knot visible in the index finger, then the man is clever, promising, prudent and is capable of being successful in his objective.

2. If there is knot on the lower side of the finger of Saturn, then the man will repeatedly get failure in his work. On the contrary, if only the upper knot is visible, then the man is determined and does not get disheartened even when he becomes unsuccessful. If both the knots are visible in the finger of Saturn, then it can safely be said that he will get rapid success and rapid failure in business. If there is no knot available in the finger of Saturn, then such a person is stable, sober and very learned or a big businessman and will succeed in supporting hundreds of persons.

3. If the knot is visible in the lower part of the finger of Apollo, then the man will be weak in religious matters. He is less interested in religious matters. If the knot is visible only in the upper part, then such a person fears religion and is weak-hearted. If both the knots are visible in the finger of Apollo, then such a person is anti-social and anti-religious. He has no regard for religion or social work in his life. Such a person is totally selfish and is engrossed in his own welfare. On the contrary, if there are no knots visible in the finger of Apollo, such persons are able to lead the society and their contribution towards the society is clearly felt. There is a distinct aim in their work. They are specially mindful about the welfare of others rather than their own selfish ends. Such persons can give correct direction to the society.
4. If the knot is on the lower side of the finger of Mercury, then the person is found to be very clever and careful. He is adept in breaking the law and is a leader in anti-social activities. If the knot is found on the upper part of the finger of Mercury, then such a person is found to be helpful to the society and a greater part of his life is spent in social work. If there are two knots available in the little finger, then such a person can certainly not remain neutral. In addition to being selfish, such a person is engrossed in wrong works. Society should not hope much from such a man. Persons having no knots on the small finger have ideal life. Their ideas are pure and pious and they are able to give something new to the society. Such persons are called 'jewels' of the society.
5. There is only one knot in the thumb because there are only two parts in a thumb. If the knot in the thumb is visible, then such persons are weak-hearted and they are generally unconcerned towards their duties. Conversely, if no knot is seen on a thumb, then the person is firm in taking decisions and has unfailing faith in his work. He makes all efforts to bring the work to completion once he makes up his mind to do it. Firmness, strong will and unfailing faith to do a work is deeply rooted in his life. Such persons become successful in giving a new leadership to the society and the nation.

◆◆

The Thumb and Fingers

Thumb, in a way, represents the whole hand. More importance is attached to the thumb than it is given to the lines on the palm. Just as a man's face is a reflection of his life, similarly, the thumb reveals the whole individuality of a person to the palmist. The thumb is considered as the root of the whole hand. The importance of fingers without the thumb becomes negligible. The thumb alone keeps the full power of the whole hand and gives strength to do the work. At the time of birth, a baby's thumb appears almost covered with his four fingers. As such, palmistry has accepted the significance of the thumb as of paramount importance.

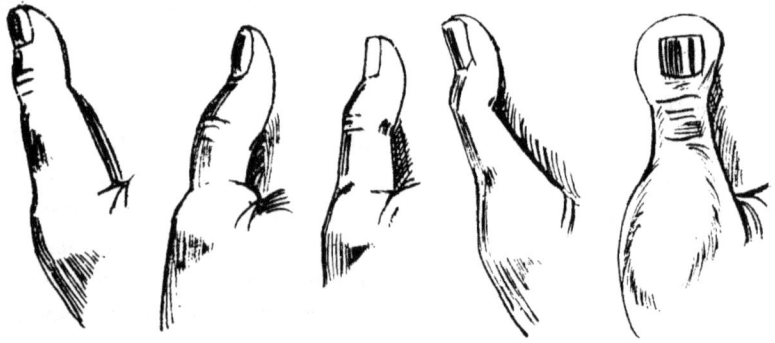

The thumb is considered as the centre of the will-power. It is formed with two pieces of bones. Two bones projecting from the palm are clearly visible and the third forms the inner part of the palm, which is called the mount of Venus and this part is considered to be the centre of passion and love. The first phalange of the thumb indicates logic and the phalange containing the nail indicates will-power.

The thumb makes the internal activity of a person clear and has direct connection with the mind. As the mind is acknowledged to be supreme in a human body, therefore, a man's nature, his character and his ideas can be studied by looking only at the thumb. According to medical science, no harm is done if all the four fingers of a person are cut off but if for some reason, the thumb is torn and there is profuse bleeding, then the person may go insane and several times, it results in his death. From this small fact, the importance of thumb can be judged.

The human thumb can be divided into three kinds taking into consideration the atmosphere and the different climates.

1 —Thumbs which make an obtuse angle in conjunction with the index finger of the palm.

2 —Thumbs which make a right angle in conjunction with the index finger.

3 —Thumbs which form an acute angle in conjunction with the index finger on the palm.

I am giving a brief description of these three kinds of thumbs for the convenience of the readers.

1. Obtuse-angled Thumb: Such thumbs are well-formed, long and thin. These are called gentle thumbs. Persons having such thumbs on their palms are gentle and sweet-tempered. They are artists and musicians and do practical and useful work in society. Though the childhood of such persons has been full of struggles, still they succeed in making the homely environment favourable with their own efforts and rise high even though they have to face obstacles and struggles constantly but they succeed in their lives due to their strong will-power.

An extraordinarily long thumb is considered inauspicious. If the length of the thumb exceeds the second phalange of the index finger, then such a person is a fool and cannot succeed in life. If the length of the thumb is ordinary and proportionate, then the person is wise, clever and lover of arts. Such a person gives priority to the service of humanity and community than his ownself. Though the number of friends in their lives is less, still irrespective of number, all friends help at the time of need. His mind is unstable. Such persons go on changing their minds again and again and succeed only in life after overcoming numerous obstacles.

2. Right-angled Thumb: These are those thumbs which form a right angle with the index finger. These thumbs are elegant, strong and appear like pillars but such thumbs are not leaning towards the rear.

Such thumbs, if seen carefully, reveal that the person believes more in doing work and labour rather than in useless gossip. Though they are of very short temperament, yet it is seen that they cool down as quickly as they get angry. It is true that they sit quietly when they are angry and don't harm anyone. They strictly stick to their words. At times, they stick to wrong things which create problems. The feeling of revenge is so strong in them that they don't forget the enmity for several generations. Such persons can either be good friends or good enemies.

Such persons get broken in their lives but yielding is beyond them. If seen in correct perspective, such persons are patriots, are prepared to sacrifice their lives for the country or society and are strong-minded. Once they make up their mind to do certain things, they surely do it. They don't like to play a second fiddle and so they are guided by their ownselves.

3. Acute-angled Thumb: Thumbs which make an acute angle at the joint with the index finger come under this category. The length of such thumbs is comparatively less and they are clumsy to look at. Such thumbs are classed as of evil quality.

Persons with this kind of thumb generally have frustrating feelings in their lives. Their life abounds in laziness. They have no liking for journeys, etc. and do not believe in completing any work thoroughly. Such thumbs are often seen in middle-and low-class persons. They remain busy in bad habits and evil deeds which result in extravagance in comparison to their earning. They waste money much more than necessary and pass their lives in dreaming for unobtainable objects. They are less interested in religion or pious actions. They are somewhat inclined towards ghosts, spirits, gods and goddesses, etc. and take pleasure in deeds of low standards.

Such persons are licentious and are always attracted towards other women. They remain in constant contact with women of low class and get defamed several times in their lives. In my opinion, society does not get any benefit from such persons.

THREE PARTS OF A THUMB

By observing carefully, it can be found that the thumb is divided into three main parts. First part is one at which the nail is stuck. The second is the middle part and third one is joined to the mount of Venus on the palm. According to the science of palmistry, the first phalange is indicative of good (Sat), the second of mediocre (Raj) and the third of evil (Tam). We call the upper portion as first phalange or first "Ardha Bhaga", the middle portion as second phalange or the middle part and the lower portion as the lower part. The upper portion is indicative of science and will-power, the middle portion shows the logic and thinking capacity while the third portion denotes love, attraction and affection.

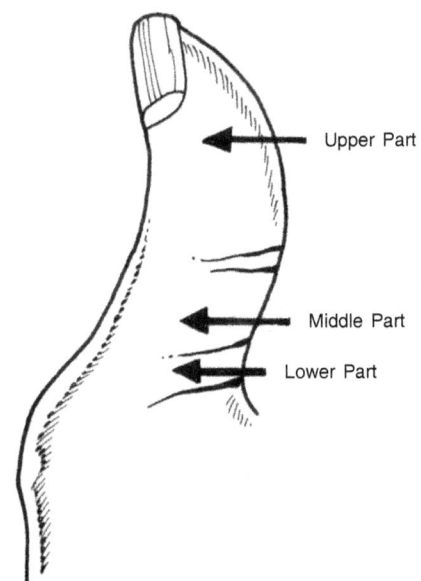

Three Main Parts of A Thumb

The First Phalange

A person whose first part is longer than the second part has strong will-power and is independent in taking decisions. Such persons are not able to do a work under the subordination of another person. Such persons have deep faith in religious ideas and their own individuality is so attractive and strong that a man gets influenced as soon as he sees him. They are able to get anything done on the strength of their personality. Such persons are more satisfied and happy in old age rather than in young age.

These persons succeed in getting respectable position in the society if their first and second phalanges are equally long and thick. They neither cheat anyone nor are they cheated easily by anyone. They have many friends in life and such people are very popular in the society. They are seen smiling even under difficulties or in adverse conditions.

The Second Phalange

The second part of the thumb has been accepted as the place for power of logic (reasoning). If the second phalange is bigger and stronger than the first, it is proved that the man possesses adequate reasoning and the speciality of the man will be that he will not let anyone stand before him in reasoning. But such persons have one weakness that they try to get just and unjust things accepted by reasoning. If they find their side is lacking in reasoning, then they try to prove their version by making hue and cry. They do not get much respect in a civilized society and they are called talkative. If this phalange is thin, such persons blurt out anything without using their minds. Such persons remain busy in finding fault in their officers and their life is a burden to them.

If the first and second phalanges are equal in length, width and thickness, then such persons are said to be cool-minded. Neither do they get angry easily nor are they puffed up in praise by momentary excitement. They take every step in life with care with the result that they have to face the least amount of cheating. They have absolute self-confidence. To draw a correct picture of these persons or to describe them in correct words, one can say that they are cultured businessmen of high calibre, hold very high and responsible posts in government and are acknowledged artists.

Persons whose second phalange is thinner and weaker in comparison with the first phalange are those who do not work with their own minds but like to work under the guidance of others. In fact, they cannot take any decision independently. They do any work in life without planning, which always results in failure at the end. Their soul is weak. They are fickle-minded and quarrelsome by nature and they can be classed as unsuccessful persons in life.

In fact, such persons believe in destiny and, at the same time, they are lazy too.

The Third Part of the Thumb

The third part of the thumb is not called phalange, instead it is the place of Venus. The mount of Venus has been explained at appropriate place in this book.

This part certainly is more prominent, firm and elegant. A person, whose this part is more prominent than usual, elegant and has pink tinge, is well advanced in love matters and affection. Such persons receive respect in the society and succeed in earning full popularity among friends. They remain smiling under difficulties and are bent upon succeeding in life with their own efforts.

If the mount of Venus is very protruded, then the person will be licentious and sexually immoral and will always run after beauty. He is prepared to do anything for love and beauty and, under emotion, is prepared to do anything without thinking of the consequences. If this area is submerged, or less prominent or has more than necessary lines or net on this area, then such a person is of frustrated temperament. His love is not pure love but is accompanied with lust and hidden selfishness. He makes lengthy plans and goes on dreaming but cannot get success in his aims. Lack of emotions doesn't get him full respect in society. His life is full of struggles and he has to face too many obstacles in his married life.

Fingers

I have given some hints about fingers in the previous pages. This should be borne in mind that the fingers have direct connection with the mind. If there is much load on fingers, then the blood vessels of the mind also get affected. Ordinarily, there are four fingers in each hand.

1. The Index finger
2. The finger of Saturn
3. The finger of Apollo
4. The little finger or the finger of Mercury.

Every finger from among the four fingers is divided into three parts. If seen in their natural sequence, the finger of Saturn is the

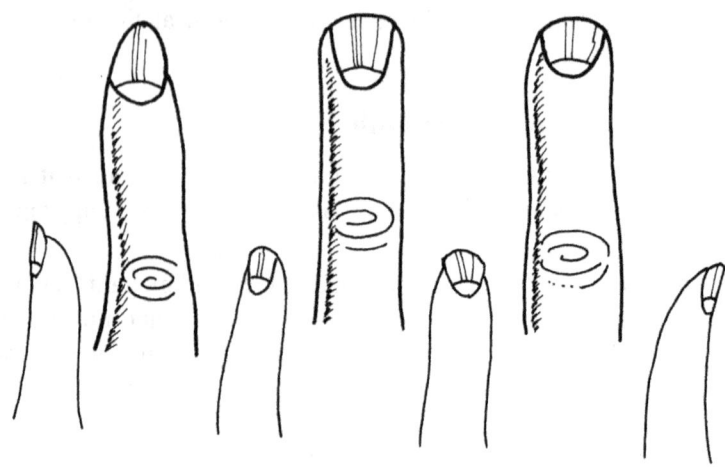

Fingers

longest; the index finger reaches the middle part of the last phalange; the finger of Apollo too is almost equally long and the little finger reaches the last phalange of the finger of Apollo. This length may be a little less or a little more, differing from individual to individual.

Index finger, the first finger is close to the thumb. The mount of Jupiter is situated at its base. The finger of Saturn is near the index finger and the mount of Saturn is situated at its base. The finger next to the finger of Saturn is called the finger of Apollo, at the root of which the mount of Apollo or the mount of Sun is situated. The finger close to the finger of Apollo is called the little finger or the finger of Mercury, at the base of which the Mount of Mercury is situated. This is the smallest of all the fingers.

The Index Finger

It is called *Tarjani* in Hindi. In most hands, this finger is smaller than the finger of Apollo. But, in some cases, I have seen this finger to be longer than the finger of Apollo. If this finger is longer than the finger of Apollo in a person's hand, then such persons are full of self-esteem, pride and occupy responsible posts. They are not interested in religious matters but they believe in flattering their superior officers. They superintend their subordinates with strictness and have too much sense of ruling others. Though they get insulted several times by the society on this account, yet they move ahead due to their patience.

If the index finger is smaller than the finger of Apollo, then such a person is clever and is expert to get his work done in anyway. Such persons should be regarded as selfish and cunning.

If the index finger is extraordinarily small, the person is adept in taking sudden decisions. If it is extraordinarily long, then the person is cruel, proud and licentious. If the index finger is long and the upper tip is pointed, then such persons are superstitious and have more than necessary faith in religion. If the finger is long but the upper tip is squarish, such persons have good moral character and are charitably disposed. If the index finger is of average length and the upper tip is flat, the person is fickle-minded. If only the first phalange of the index finger is long, then such a person can be called self-confident. If only the second phalange is long, then such a person is too much ambitious. If the third phalange is long, the person is more than enough proud and arrogant. If both finger of Apollo and the index finger of a person are equal, then such a person becomes famous in the whole world. Napolean Bonaparte and Abraham Lincoln had their both the index fingers and fingers of Apollo equal.

The Finger of Saturn

It is called *Madhyama* in Hindi. The mount of Saturn is situated at its base. Ordinarily, this finger is longer than the finger of Apollo and the index finger but this length should not be more than 1/4 of an inch. If it is more than 1/4 inch longer, then such person's whole life is full of troubles, difficulties and his wants remain unfulfilled. If the finger is longer only by just 1/4 of an inch, the person is wise, takes part in auspicious works and always makes progress. Such a person gets respect and fame in the society.

If the finger of Saturn is longer by 1/2 an inch or more from the index finger, the person will certainly be a murderer. It can be safely concluded.

If the finger of Saturn is long, the man is sickly and licentious. If this finger is fluffy and knotty in addition to being long, such a person is selfish and remains full of anxieties. If this finger is long and its tip is squarish, the person is sober and successfully discharges his duties on posts of responsibility. If this finger is long but flat at the top, such persons are specially successful in the line of art and get high regard, fame and good name through the medium of arts. A man commits suicide if the first phalange of the middle finger is long. If the second phalange is comparatively longer, then such a person succeeds in business, specially gains heavily in dealing in machines. If the third phalange is long, the person is miserly and gets defame in society. If the upper tip of the finger of Saturn is leaning towards the index finger, the person has more than necessary self-confidence and succeeds in achieving his aim or goal due to self-confidence. If its upper part is leaning towards the finger of Apollo, the person trusts his destiny and is interested in music and arts, etc.

The Finger of Apollo

In Hindi, this finger is known as *Anamika*. The mount of Sun is situated at the base of this finger. Generally, this finger is smaller than the finger of Saturn but just a little longer than the index finger. But in some hands, things contrary to this have been observed. If this finger is longer than the index finger, then such a person gets a rise in life and has plenty of kindness, love, affection and other desirable qualities. But if this finger gets equal to the finger of Saturn, then such persons are very selfish and wicked. Such persons don't hasitate to do the worst towards other people but they believe in fate and spend most of their money in gambling, speculation and other bad works. Such persons are called uncivilized and unkind. If the finger of Apollo is leaning towards the little finger, such a person earns a lot of profit from business and his whole life is spent in trade. But if this finger is leaning towards the finger of Saturn, then such a person thinks deeply and is self-centred and performs some such works in life that the society and the country remember him in future.

If the finger of Apollo is small, then such a person earns money from art, painting and old things. If the tip of such a finger is sharp or pointed, then the person is a successful musician or a painter. If the tip is squarish, then he earns wealth and fame with the help of art. If the upper part is flat, then he takes great interest with things connected with history and also gains success in them. If the first phalange of this finger is long, he has a special liking for art. If the second phalange is long, then such a person rises to a very high post due to his own genius. If the third phalange is long and wide, then he earns countywide esteem in his life. If this finger is equal to the index finger, he has a great longing for fame. If this finger is equal to the finger of Saturn, then some events occur unexpectedly in his life and he gains success ultimately.

The Finger of Mercury

It is called *Kanishthika* in Hindi. The mount of Mercury is situated at its base. Mostly, this finger is smaller than other fingers in the hand. If this finger reaches the nail of the finger of Apollo, then the person reaches a very high status in life and gets appointed on a responsible high post. The longer this finger, the more auspicious it is considered. Persons with such fingers are called successful administrators and successful men of letters. If this finger is longer than half the part of the upper phalange of the finger of Apollo, then such persons become a secretary or an I.A.S. authority. Such a person gets sudden wealth and the latter part of his life passes very successfully.

If this finger appears to be unusually long, then such persons are intellectuals and are specially gifted to impress other people. If this finger is very small, the man is able to know the underlying meaning very quickly and is capable of taking quick decisions. If the tip of the finger is pointed, then such persons are wise, quick and microscopic observers and good conversationalists. If the front tip is squarish, then such persons are specially capable of using logical decisions and impress people with their speeches. If the upper part is flat, then he becomes a scientist or takes great interest in the working of machinery. If the first phalange of this finger is long, then the person gets success in science. If the second phalange is long then he gains much in business with his own labour. If the third phalange is long, then such a person is very clever, but he has the tendency of telling lies more than necessary. If this finger is equal to the finger of Apollo in length then such a person is a philosopher and a learned man of a very high order. If this finger appears to be equal in length to the finger of Saturn, then such person becomes world-wise famous by his works. In fact, the long the finger of Mercury the more it is, considered auspicious.

Distance Between Fingers

The space between two fingers has its own significance. If there is much space between the thumb and the index finger, then such a man has adequate human values and human qualities like love, kindness, pardon, etc. and these are found in a simple natural way. If there is space between the index finger and the finger of Saturn, then such a person has independent ideas and does not hesitate to express his thoughts before others. The space between the finger of Saturn and finger of Apollo is indicative of carelessness and uncivilized attitude of a person. In the same way, if there is space between the finger of Apollo and the little finger then such a person is a murderer and cruel.

FOREPARTS OF FINGERS

The foreparts of the fingers also have great significance in future-telling. According to palmistry these foreparts are of four kinds:
1. Sharp
2. Flat
3. Pointed
4. Squarish

It has severally been observed that the foreparts of all the fingers are sometimes similar while sometimes the foreparts of different fingers are different. Now I am explaining this in a general way

1. Sharp-tipped Fingers: Persons having sharp fingers, of whose foreparts are sharp, are of high calibre and are considered leaders in the society. Such persons are philosophers, artists, musicians and work according to the dictates of their conscience. They do not have hatred, anger and thoughtlessness in them. On the other hand, their heart is full to the brim with kindness, love and affection.

But very sharp fingers are indicative of mental disorder. Such persons are lost in imagination only. They have little success in their life. Charmers have almost such sharp fingers. It has been seen and experienced that persons with sharp foreparts in their fingers are advanced and civilized.

2. Flat Fingers: Flat fingers indicate efficiency and alertness. Such persons are always busy in their work and never leave it unfinished. Unless the work is properly completed, they don't take rest. They have great self-confidence and the work reaches its completion due to their self-confidence. Such persons are successful war specialists, musicians, expert workmen, champion players and highly learned men. They have a special inclination to learn. They are orderly and systematic in their work. Such persons are not orthodox towards religion but are charitable in all walks of life. In fact, only such persons are able to contribute something to the society.

3. Pointed Fingers: These fingers indicate good ideas and good works of human beings. Anything which such persons do will be done in a systematic way and they have a proper order in their work but it has been seen that there are constant ups and downs in their lives. Sometimes they are at the pinnacle of happiness while at other times, they get badly disappointed. Their married life is generally unsuccessful. Very pointed foreparts of fingers are not considered favourable. Such persons will have less self-confidence and they work according to their emotions. Such persons are lazy, licentious and inefficient. Such persons are not able to keep secrets within themselves.

4. Squarish Fingers: Persons having squarish fingers are farsighted and work according to rules. Mostly such persons come under the category of traders who plan everything after careful thought. Such persons are careful at every step and have a systematic way of doing every work. They themselves put in full labour and know how to take work from others. Cleanliness, sticking to punctuality, fulfilling the words given, self-confidence, etc. are some of the traits specially found in them. Such persons are good mathematicians, historians and poets. Such persons can get special success in life.

STUDY OF FINGERS

If the fingers are leaning inside, then such individuals are very wise in materialistic affairs and such persons can take care of everything very carefully.

If the fingers are leaning outside, then such persons have generous hearts. They are true to their words and if ever they give any assurance to anybody in life, they stick to their words till the last breath of their lives. If the fingers are leaning too much outside, then the person is careless.

If the fingers are curved in formation and clumsy, then such persons belong to the criminal class and are interested in unlawful acts.

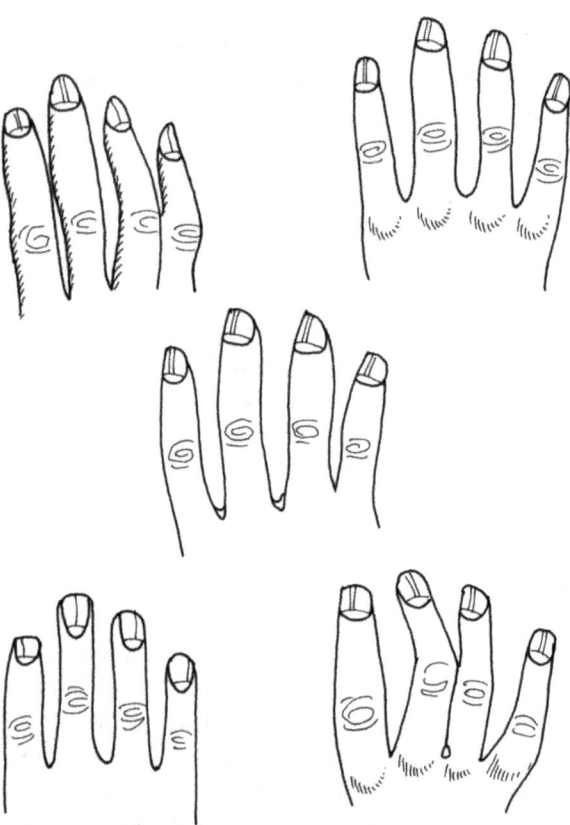

Different Types of Top-sided Fingers

Thick and clumsy fingers are indicative of poverty. Such persons spend more than they earn.

If the fingers are flat, then these persons are successful in doing service. They reach a high status and become officers of high rank and thereby get praise in society.

If the fingers are in one straight alignment, then such persons are fortunate and get special respect in society.

If all the fingers are knotty and uneven, then the person is thoughtful and fond of learning.

If the knots of fingers are very developed, then such a person is a great genius and a thinker. There is a special fineness and system in each of his work.

If these knots are very prominent, then such a person is disappointed and meets with sudden death.

If these knots are smooth, then the man is emotional, more than necessary.

If there are no knots on the fingers, then the man will be a philosopher.

SIGNS OF FINGERS

Signs found on fingers are also of great importance to a palmist. These have great significance in criminology. A person's character and his way of thinking can be known fully. His individuality can be understood with the help of these signs. These signs are of different kinds:

1. Javelin: If there is a sign of javelin or an arrow on the first phalange of the finger, the person is very capable and learned from intellectual point of view. Such persons succeed even in adverse conditions and win over such conditions. They are capable of working according to the atmosphere. Such persons succeed in life with their own efforts but in old age, they are found to be heart patients.

2. Tent: Sign like a tent is seen on the phalanges of fingers of some persons. Such persons are generally kind-hearted and rise very high by means of their art. This is also true that people take undue advantage of such persons. Such persons are unbalanced mentally and their family life is generally troublesome.

3. Circle: Sign of circles on fingers is considered auspicious. Such persons are independent in their thoughts and originality is seen in all that they do. They get honour on the strength of their judgement and remain away from old beliefs, ignorance and conservatism.

4. Arch: Persons with arch on their fingers are generally lazy and of suspicious nature. Such persons have no confidence in themselves nor do they trust others. Such persons create an atmosphere of illusion around them. They gain special success in mystic works and detective services.

5. Triangle: The sign of triangle makes a man mysterious. Such persons are able to make their bodies strong by practising Yoga. At the same time, such persons love loneliness and are orthodox. They do not leave a thing once it gets into their mind.

6. Star: Persons, on whose fingers the sign of star or cross is visible, are very fateful and fortunate. Such persons receive wealth in life quite unexpectedly many times. They remain happy from financial point of view in life.

7. Circle: If a circular sign is seen in the phalanges of fingers, then the person is an ideal lover and ideal friend. On one side, they are desirous of amorous activities, while on the other hand, they are inclined towards asceticism. They are fickle-minded and it is not their nature to complete any work in its full.

8. Net: Fingers with nets on them are indicative that the man will meet more than necessary obstacles and difficulties in life. Their life-power is firm and they come out unscathed from difficulties due to their will-power. Even then they are less comfortable and less happy in life. Such signs are easily seen on the fingers of culprits and dacoits.

9. Rectangle: If a rectangle is seen on the phalange of the finger, then it should be understood that the person is laborious in his life and is capable of keeping the Goddess of wealth under his own power and efforts. Such a person is prosperous from financial point of view and is happy.

If more than one sign is seen on the finger of a person, then the person is entitled to the combined benefits of those signs.

THUMB

Much can be known from the thumb of a person. Hence, I am throwing light in this connection also:

1. Long Thumb: Such persons are self-willed, self-dependent and control others. In their lives, intelligence has more importance than emotions and in this way, they can be called intellectuals. They are specially interested in mathematics and engineering.

2. Short Thumb: Such persons don't work with their own mind but do so under the influence of others. Emotions have a prominent place in their lives than intelligence. They take special interest in poetry, painting, music, etc.

3. Hard Thumb: Such persons are obstinate and alert. They possess the capacity to keep anything to themselves. They are wanting in emotions in their lives and they mostly work on the strength of intelligence.

4. Flexible and Supple Thumb: A person with such a thumb is much interested in amassing wealth and is capable of adjusting himself according to the circumstances.

5. The First Phalange of the Thumb: If the first phalange of the thumb is very long, then such a person is self-willed, while he has less desire to work if the thumb is shorter. Such persons are weak-willed. If the forepart of the thumb is squarish, the person is clever in legal matters and is highly respected for his acts of justice and fairness. He is very obstinate if the forepart of the thumb is wide. He gets harmed several times in life due to his being obstinate. If the forepart of the thumb is extraordinarily long, then such a person is a murderer or a dacoit or remains engrossed in anti-social activities.

6. The Second Phalange of the Thumb: Persons, whose second phalange is long, are clever, careful and take a leading part in social works. He is held in high esteem in society due to his works. If this phalange is short, the person does work without thinking and repents constantly if he becomes unsuccessful. He invariably takes part in works full of danger. If this phalange is clumsy, then he is devoid of the power of reasoning. If this phalange is depressed, then the person's mind is sharp and sensitive. In true sense, the study of thumb and fingers has a great significance in itself for a palmist.

Mount

Mounts have a special significance in the study of palms because different lines are formed and developed due to mounts. Mounts have been named after the names of 'planets' and the special features of the planets are revealed by the prominence of mounts. For example, the Sun or Apollo is responsible for respect, fame, praise, etc. Therefore, if the mount of Sun is prominent on the palm, then the person will certainly get special respect and status. But, if the mount of Sun is not prominent on the palm, then such a person cannot get the desired respect and praise irrespective of the high status he attains.

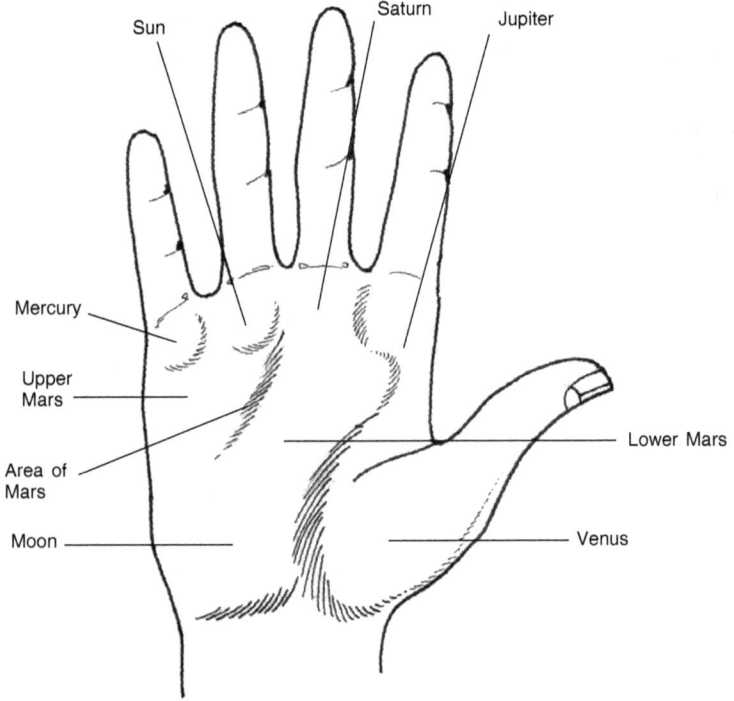

The Place of Mounts on Palm

It has been found by experience that the planet which is prominent in the horoscope is also found prominent on the palm, that is, its mount is clear and well-shaped. In a way, there is no difference in planets of the horoscope and the mounts on the palm. Therefore, it is said that a horoscope can be prepared after studying the lines and mounts on a palm.

MOUNTS ARE OF THREE KINDS

1. Ordinary Mounts.
2. Well-developed Mounts
3. Underdeveloped Mounts.

If the mounts on a palm are sufficiently prominent, muscular, healthy and reddish, then they are called developed mounts. Contrary to it, underdeveloped mounts are generally not visible. Ordinary mounts are those which neither come under developed category nor can be accepted as well-developed mounts.

The planets, their Hindi names and corresponding influences are as follows:

1. The Mount of Jupiter: It is called *Brihaspati* or *Guru* in Hindi. It is a benevolent planet and it is connected with government service, show of desires, etc.

2. The Mount of Saturn: It is called *Shani* in Hindi and it is connected with meditation, loneliness, disease, anxiety, business and machinery, etc.

3. The Mount of Apollo or Sun: It is called *Surya* in Hindi language. Government service, mental advancement, fame, respect, praise and miscellaneous arts and crafts are studied by means of this planet.

4. The Mount of Mercury: It is called *Budh* in Hindi. Advancement of science, trade, mathematical works, are studied with the help of this planet.

5. The Mount of Harshal: It is called *Prajapati* in Hindi. It is connected with physical and mental capabilities.

6. The Mount of Neptune: In Hindi, it is called *Varun*. A person's learning, his individuality, his influence upon others and his courage, etc. are known by means of this mount.

7. The Mount of Moon or Luna: It is called *Chandra* in Hindi. This mount on the palm helps in the study of imagination, large-heartedness, sympathy, mental rise and voyages across the sea.

8. The Mount of Venus: It is called *Shukra* in Hindi. Beauty, love grandeur, splendour and enjoyment, etc. are studied by the means of this mount.

9. The Mount of Mars: It is called *Mangal* in Hindi. War, courage, energy, hard work, man-like qualities, etc. are studied by the means of this mount.

10. The Mount of Dragon's Head: It is called *Rahu* in Hindi. This planet is connected with obtaining sudden wealth, lottery, heart attack or sudden happenings.

11. The Mount of Dragon's Tail: It is caller *Ketu* in Hindi. Wealth, material prosperity and bank balance are studied with the help of this mount.

12. The Mount of Pluto: It is called *Indra* in Hindi. This mount reveals mental thinking and spiritual advancement.

AREAS OF THE PLANETS

The exact places of all the planets are fixed in palmistry and by looking at these minutely, they can be recognised.

1. The Mount of Jupiter: It is situated at the base of the index finger and above the mount of Mars. It is considered by its very nature-God of power, leadership, organisation and authorship. The mount of Jupiter reveals these facts clearly.

If the mount of Jupiter is well developed and prominent, then such a person is said to possess godly qualities. While such person advances himself, he is helpful in raising others as well. Such persons try to save their self-respect specially. They are learned, just, always prepared to help others and act according to the words given, are benevolent and are highly respected in society. They don't get disturbed even under most difficult conditions. Infact, all the justices of high courts and high authorities, etc. must have a well developed mount of Jupiter. Such persons have the special quality of changing the public in their favour and are more than necessary religious-minded.

If the mount of Jupiter is less prominent or underdeveloped, then there is a general deficiency of the above qualities in a person. Physically such persons are of ordinary body, healthy and have smiling faces. They are experts in reading and delivering lectures, are kind at heart and benefactors. They are more inclined towards the attainment of respect and good reputation rather than wealth. They have special qualities of authority, independence and leadership.

They have soft corner for persons of the other sex and have very cordial relations with beautiful and civilized ladies. If this mount is well-developed on the palms of females, they have the desire to submit or yield to others.

If the mount of Jupiter is leaning towards the mount of Saturn, then such a person remains busy with his own works but fails to get success in life. So he gradually begins to become frustrated. By nature, they are serious and obstinate. If the mount of Jupiter is in lower position, the person has to face defame several times in his life, but gets complete success in the line of literary pursuits.

If the mount of Jupiter is developed more than necessary, then such a person is found to be selfish, proud and self-willed.

If the mount of Jupiter, is absent in a person, there is want of self-respect in him. They get very little patronage from their parents but they are generally found in the company of persons of low ideas and of lower category.

If the protrusion of this mount is general and good, the man has a desire to go ahead but he gets married in an early age and his family life is generally happy.

If the fingers are pointed and the mount of Jupiter is well developed, then such a person is superstitious. Similarly, if the fingers are squarish, combined with well-developed mount of Jupiter, then the person is self-willed and cruel in life, in a way. If the fingers are very long and the mount of Jupiter is developed, then the person will be extravagant and licentious. If the mounts of Jupiter and Saturn are equally prominent and have intermingled in one another, then such a person is very fortunate and gets special success in life.

In fact, the mount of Jupiter is said to be very helpful in life and moves a person towards progress.

2. The Mount of Saturn: It has its base at the root of the finger of Saturn. The development of this mount on the palm is indicative of extraordinary tendencies. If this mount is absent in the palm of a person, then he will not be able to get special success or respect in life.

The finger of Saturn is called the deity of good luck because the fate line ends at the base of this finger. If the mount of Saturn is fully developed, then the person is highly fortunate and rises very high in life with his own efforts. As a result of a prominent mount, such a person likes to remain aloof and constantly move forward towards his goal. He gets so much engrossed in his work and in his goal that he does not care for his household and his family. By nature, they are irritating and suspicious. With the advance in age, they become more mysterious. Persons with prominent mount of Saturn are wizards, engineers, scientists, literary men or chemists. Such persons are thrifty in their lives and believe in having more immovable property. They have less inclination towards music and dancing. They are suspicious by nature from their early childhood and look with suspicion on their own sons and wives.

If this mount is very much developed, then the person commits suicide in his life. This mount is very prominent in the hands of dacoits, cheats and robbers. The mount of such persons is generally yellowish or pale. Their palm and skin are pale and irritability is clearly seen in their nature.

If the mount of Saturn is leaning towards the mount of Jupiter, then it gives suspicious indications. Such persons get a respectable place in the society and are held in high esteem in the society. If the mount of Saturn is leaning towards the mount of Sun, then such persons are lazy, poor and remain too much dependent upon fate. They have more than necessary frustration and they see the gloomy picture in every work. They are not able to get any help from relatives and often sustain loss in business.

If there are more than necessary lines on the mount of Saturn, then such a person is coward and very licentious. If the mount of Saturn and the mount of Mercury both are developed, then such a person becomes a successful physician or a businessman. He never lacks money.

If the mount of Saturn is missing in the palm, then such a person's life has no importance. If this mount is protruded ordinarily, then the person has more than necessary faith in fate and does not succeed in his plans. Such persons have very few friends; they are obstinate by nature and are non-religious.

If the tip of the finger of Saturn is pointed and the mount of Saturn is prominent, the person likes to be imaginative. But if the tip of the finger is squarish, the person makes spectacular progress in the field of agriculture or chemistry.

3. The Mount of Sun or Apollo: The mount of sun is situated at the base of the finger of Apollo and on the upper part of the Heart line. This mount is indicative of the success of the individual. If there is absence of the mount of Sun in a person's hand, he leads a very ordinary life. Therefore, a person who has no mount of Sun on his palm, leads an anonymous life.

The development of this mount is very essential for the progress of a person and with the prominence of this mount, the man becomes a genius and famous. A person reaches a very high status in life if this mount is quite prominent, developed and is pink in colour. Such persons are of cheerful nature and work in close co-operation with friends. Their words and actions become news and they are very popular in general public. Such persons are successful artists, expert musicians and painters. They are inborn genius. They are honest in their dealings with others and are desirous of leading life in a grand style. If seen in correct perspective, such persons earn a lot in business and they have more than one source of income in life. They are completely materialistic and are capable to reach the bottom of the heart of the man facing them. If this mount is prominent in the hands of an illiterate or ordinary person, even then the person will be wealthy and prosperous. They receive unexpected wealth several times in their lives and their mode of living is royal and full of grandeur.

They are clean-hearted and never hesitate in acknowledging their mistakes. As they are clear-headed, they can never tolerate their opposition and believe in frankly telling the bare naked truth in front of the person. It is such persons who reach responsible posts and are able to perform some original work.

If there is no mount of Sun in anybody's palm, he is dull-minded and a fool. If this mount is not prominent, then the person, though interested in beauty, is not able to succeed fully in his affairs. Very good, well-developed mount of Sun is indicative of self-confidence, gentlemanliness, kindness, generousness, wealth and grandeur. Such persons have the special quality of influencing people in meetings, etc. They are higly respected.

If this mount is developed more than necessary, then such a person will be very proud and is a flatterer. Friends of such persons are of low class. They are extravagant and quarrel on trivial matters. Such persons cannot get full success in their lives.

If the mount of Sun is leaning towards the mount of Saturn, then such a person likes to remain aloof and is full of frustration. They are always short of money in their lives. They commence any work with full zeal but they are not able to complete it with the same zeal and enthusiasm. They take up some other work and leave the former undone. In fact, the mount of sun leaning towards the mount of Saturn is indicative of bad luck.

If this mount is leaning towards the mount of Mercury, then the person will be a successful trader and very wealthy. Such persons are able to get respectable place in society.

If the finger of Apollo is clumsy, then it minimises the characteristics of the Sun. Such persons become revengeful and do not remain careful in their behaviour with others. If there are too many lines on the mount of Sun, then the person generally remains sick. If the finger of Apollo has conical tip and the mount of Sun is prominent, then such a person is much interested in arts. Squarish tips are indicative of behavioural expertise while the pointed ones are indicative of idealism.

4. The Mount of Mercury: The prominent part on the base of the finger of Mercury is called the mount of Mercury. This mount shows materialistic prosperity and affluence. Therefore, there is much importance attached to this mount these days. Persons under the influence of Mercury are able to successfully complete any work they take in hand. These persons have sharp intelligence with fertile minds and are able to understand the situations very well. Any work they do in their life is done with careful planning and any work which they commence has got to be completed.

Too much protrusion of the mount of Mercury cannot be termed beneficial. Persons with greatly developed mount of Mercury are clever and crafty and such persons are adept in cheating others. If the mount of Mercury is ordinarily developed and has a mark of square on it, then such a person will be a criminal of a very high order. Such persons believe in breaking the law, are fickle-minded and are experts in indulging in anti-social activities.

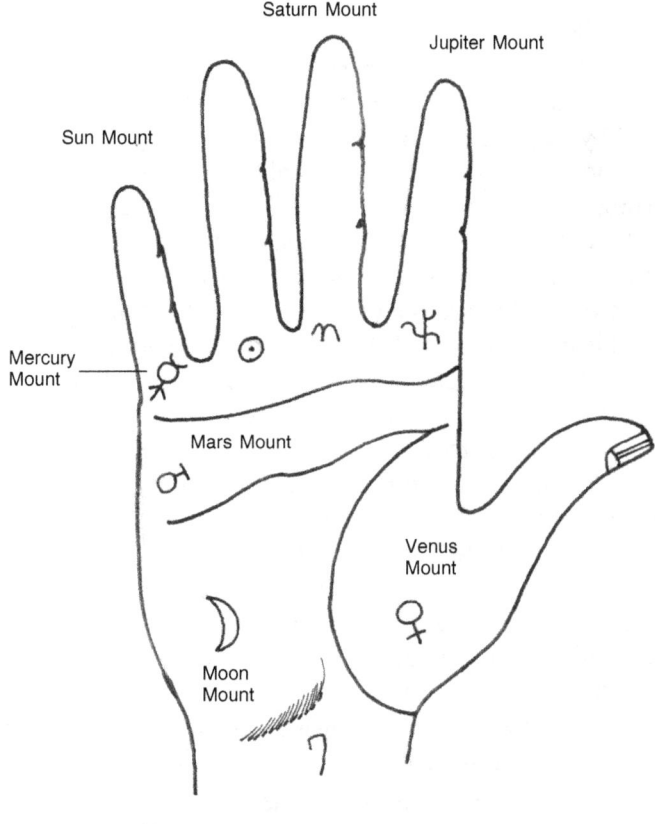

Mounts

Persons, in whose hands the mount of Mercury is prominent, are experts in psychology and they know very well how to influence a person. Such persons gain much success in business.

If the mount of Mercury is prominent in a hand, such a person is an opportunist and is always in search of the right time. He or She is considered clever in taking advantage of any opportunity. Such persons are successful speakers.

In one way, such persons are fully materialistic. They don't think of fair or foul means of amassing wealth and take special interest in philosophy, science, mathematics etc.. Such persons become eminent pleaders, fine speakers and successful actors in their lives.

Such persons gain fame in literary pursuits also. They are fond of journeys and wandering is their pet hobby. Such persons gain full success in their lives.

If the mount of Mercury is very much protruded, then such persons are mad after money and the main aim of their life is to amass money by any means. If this mount is leaning towards the mount of Apollo, then such persons are able to get success in life easily. Such mounts are seen in the hands of literary men and scientists, etc. If the palm of any person is supple and the mount of Mercury is fully prominent over it, then such a person amasses lakhs of rupees by his own efforts. If this mount is absent on the palm, then the person passes his life in poverty. If the mount of Mercury is ordinarily prominent, then he is interested in inventions and scientific work. If the tip of the little finger is pointed and the mount of Mercury is prominent, then such a person is a very clever conversationalist. If the tip is squarish, then the person has much reasoning power. Flat tip lends special efficiency in eloquence. If the little finger is small, the person has sharp intelligence. If the mount of Mercury is accompanied with long fingers, then such a person is very fond of women. If the finger is knotty, then such a person is firm-minded. If the fingers of the hand are long and leaning backward, then such a person succeeds very well in cheating. If the mount of Mercury is leaning outside the palm, then he succeeds well in business. If it is prominent and complete in itself, then such a person gains full success in life.

5. The Mount of Venus: The spot beneath the second phalange of the thumb and surrounded by the age line is called the mount of Venus by palmists. In Greece, 'Venus' is said to be the Goddess of beauty. Persons having the mount of Venus of a high order are beautiful and perfectly civilized. Such persons are very healthy and are able to influence a person by their personality. Such persons do not lack courage. If this mount is less prominent in any person's hand, then he is a coward and weak-natured.

Persons with very prominent mount of Venus are licentious and always covet for the opposite sex. If there is absence of this mount in any hand, then he lives like an ascetic or a mendicant or a recluse and has no interest in family life. If the mount of Venus is fully prominent but his head line is not balanced, then such a person gets bad name in love affairs and sex matters. The love of such person is predominant with sex.

The prominence of the mount of Venus makes a man brilliant and handsome. He has such an attractive face that people are automatically attracted towards such a person. They face difficulties smilingly and are always alert about their duties and responsibilities. They have a natural inclination towards beautiful and artistic things.

If the palm is coarse and the mount of Venus is very prominent, then the person is sexy and licentious. Such persons are slaves of worldy pleasures, but if the palm is smooth and soft and the mount of Venus is very prominent on it, then such a person is a successful lover and an eminent poet.

Absence of the mount of Venus fills a person's life with troubles and miseries. If the mount of Venus is ordinarily prominent, then the person will have a sense of beautiful pure love and will be sensitive. He does not behave delicately in the sphere of love if the mount of Venus is leaning towards the mount of Mars. There are many rape cases in his life.

Persons with prominent mount of Venus specially suffer from diseases of the throat. Such persons do not have any faith in God. In their lives, they have a large number of friends and they think love and beauty to be the be-all and end-all of everything.

If the tip of the thumb is conical and the mount of Venus is prominent, then the person has an artistic taste. If the tip of the thumb is squarish, then such a person is considered to be wise and acts after careful consideration. A flat thumb fills a man with thoughts of kindness.

In fact, only the persons with prominent mount of Venus can recognise the world and enjoy it properly.

6. The Mount of Mars: There are two Mars on the palms. They are known as *Progressive Mars* and *Regressive Mars*.

Surrounded portion beneath the starting point of the lifeline and above the mount of Venus is called the mount of Mars. Basically, this mount is indicative of war. Persons with prominent mount of Mars are courageous, fearless and powerful.

Persons with a prominent mount of Mars are brave. They are neither cowards nor can be easily subdued. Such persons have firmness and balance in their lives. A person can be considered a coward if the mount of Mars is absent in his palm.

Persons having a prominent mount of Mars are tall and muscular. Steadiness and courage are special qualities of these persons. They cannot tolerate the least injustice in their lives. Such persons reach a very high position in police or in army. They have the in-born quality of administration and such persons are competent leaders of society.

A person turns out to be a villain, tyrant and a criminal if the mount of Mars is very prominent. He is always ahead of all in anti-social activities. He is quarrelsome by nature. He is in the habit of getting his opinion followed by force. Such persons are ready to fight on the slightest pretext. They sacrifice everything to obtain their rights and are perfect liars and crafty persons.

It may be understood for certain that a man has more evils than good qualities if the mount of Mars is leaning towards the mount of Venus. Not only this but there will also be a very high intensity of every feeling. If such persons are inimical, they will be arch-enemies but in case they are friendly disposed, they will be prepared to sacrifice everything. Such persons are ostentatious, fond of pomp and show, and pretentious display. They are adept at getting their work done by giving false threats though they are cowards at heart themselves.

In truth, such persons are impolite and harsh. If lines are specially visible on the mount of Mars, it can be safely said that the person is of bellicose nature. In times to come, such a person either becomes a commander in the army or a fierce dacoit. If encouraged, they are prepared to sacrifice everything. Triangle, rectangle or any other sign on the mount of Mars is not considered auspicious. Such signs clearly indicate the sickness of the man, and diseases of the blood are present throughout their life.

If the mount of Mars is quite developed and the palm is of redish colour, then such a person is certain to reach a high position. He gets complete success in reaching his object notwithstanding struggles and obstacles in his life. Yellow colour shows a tendency towards crime. If the colour of the palm is a bit bluish, then such a person is a sufferer of rheumatism.

Such persons are ambitious and they always keep their aim in mind. They go on moving forward incessantly towards their goal. If they begin some kind of calling, they can get special success in dealing in medicines and drugs.

A person likes to be idealistic if the mount of Mars is prominent and the fingers are angular. Squarish fingers denote that the person will be too cautious in his life in dealing with others. Such persons are clever and crafty and keep a special eye for their own good. A person works with reasoning and consideration if the fingers are knotty and the mount of Mars is prominent. A man certainly meets his end in war while fighting or by a knife-thrust, if there is a cross sign found on the mount of Mars. A man will surely die in accident if zig-zag lines are found forming a net on the mount of Mars.

In fact, a man becomes courageous, fearless and frank by the presence of the mount of Mars.

7. The Mount of Luna or the Mount of Moon: Moon is the nearest planet of a man, consequently it wields the greatest influence on human beings. Correctly speaking, this planet is called the planet of beauty and imagination.

The mount of Moon or the area of Moon is formed on the palm on the left of the lifeline and below the bracelet, also below the area of Neptune where it joins the lifeline is the area of the Moon. Persons with a developed mount of Moon are delicate, emotional and romantic.

Persons with fully developed mount of Moon are lovers of nature and beauty. Such persons generally remain in dream world rather than in actual world. There is no lack of imagination in their lives. In this way, they are lost in their ownselves. They are not able to face the difficulties and struggles of life and get perturbed when confronted with slight difficulties.

Such persons are known to live a peaceful life and remain unconcerned with the deceptions of the world. Such persons are high-class artists, musicians and men of letters. They are full of religious ideas. They don't do anything under pressure and they have clear and independent ideas.

Persons, not having the mount of Moon on their palms, are hard-hearted and fully materialistic. Those who have fighting as trait in their lives, have no mount of Moon in their hands.

Persons with fully developed mount of Moon are imaginative instead of being materialistic. Love and beauty are their weaknesses but their love affair is not happy as they are not able to understand the duplicity and wickedness of the world. If the mount of Moon is very prominent, then such a person becomes a lunatic.

A person is imaginative and makes castles in the air if the mount of Moon is fairly developed. He makes plans involving crores of rupees lying on his bed but none of these is completed or, to say in other words, he has not the courage and capacity to complete these.

Such persons are too emotional. They are touched by even a slight happening. The slightest sarcasm shakes them thoroughly. Such persons hardly have any sense of struggling. They beg farewell in adverse conditions and slowly frustration occupies its home in their minds.

If the mount of Moon is prominent and leans outside, then the person has love of pleasures. Such persons become indulgent, licentious and sexy and go on chasing beautiful women uselessly. The main aim in their life is sex-enjoyment and licentiousness but even this pleasure is denied to them in life. In addition to being licentious, they are shameless also if this mount is seen leaning towards the mount of Venus on the palm. Thay can't distinguish between themselves and others and, as a result, get defamed in the society.

A person goes on voyages several times if zig-zag lines are seen on the mount of Moon. If there is a circle on the mount of Moon, then such a person will go out to foreign countries on political grounds. A person is unfriendly and fully materialistic if there is absence of the mount of Moon. If the mount of Moon is ordinarily prominent, then such a person is internally very beautiful and quite understanding. If this protrusion is on the upper side, he is afflicted by diseases like rheumatism or colds. If this mount is more than necessarily developed, then that person is found to be fickle-minded, suspicious, frustrated or nearly mad. He suffers from headache all the time. If this mount is leaning a little downwards, then such a person is physically weak. If conchshell sign is found on the mount of Moon, then the person succeeds with his own efforts but he invariably faces difficulties and obstacles. Such a person believes in leading life in a correct way and in co-operating and helping others.

In fact, the presence of the mount of Moon on a palm makes a man imaginative, lover of beauty and emotional.

8. Harshala: In fact, this planet is more powerful and exerts more influence in comparison with other planets. It has its area of influence on the palm between the Heart and Head lines. Its area of influence can be clearly seen a little below the little finger and the mount of Mercury.

A person makes wonderful advancement and gains, worldwide fame and respect if there is a triangular or square sign on this mount. He is highly respected in society and gets more success in life than expected. A person becomes famous throughout the world if a line comes from Harshal and goes towards the finger of Apollo. In case the mount of Harshal is leaning towards the mount of Mars, the person makes misuse of his genius and in a way, he becomes an international swindler or plunderer. Such a person remains constantly sick with heart trouble. If the mount of Harshal is seen leaning towards the mount of Neptune, the person is completely indulgent and goes on chasing other women and is not satisfied with his wife. In a way, his family life gets spoiled and he has no love for his children and wife. He loses his health and beauty by being too indulgent in life.

9. The Mount of Neptune: The planet is stationed at a very great distance from earth; hence, it exerts very little influence on the inhabitants of the earth but whatever little influence it exerts on a man's life, is of a permanent nature and shows wonderful results in itself.

The area of this planet on the palm is below the head line and above the area of the mount of Moon. A man becomes an eminent, musician, poet or writer if this mount or its area is very prominent. If a line is seen on this mount and this line meets the fate line a little ahead, the person gets some post of great importance.

If this mount has a tendency to lean more towards the mount of Moon, then the standard of a person by itself is of very low calibre and of low mentality and he indulges in anti-social activities.

If a line starts from the Neptune and cuts the Head line, then such a person certainly becomes insane and the greater part of his life passes in a lunatic asylum.

If this mount is developed more than enough, then such a person's life is full of grief and his family life is spoilt. Such persons are maniac, suspicious and cruel. If the mount of Neptune is developed and meets the mount of Harshal, then it can be understood that the person will surely commit murder in order to obtain wealth. Such persons are careless about their own works but repent after it has been completed.

He passes his whole life in poverty and destitution if a cross is found on this mount. Such persons cannot collect even the basic needs of life.

10. The Mount of Pluto: It is called *Indra* in Hindi. Its area on the palm is below the heart line and above the head line and is situated between the mounts of Harshal and Jupiter. This mount can be clearly seen on the hand of every person.

Its influence can be seen only in old age. If this mount is very prominent, then the person passes his old age happily and very successfully. He begins to feel happy from the age of 42 onwards and remains happy in every way till his death. If a cross sign is found on this mount, the person will die before the age of 45 in an accident.

If the mount is too prominent, the person is rude, illiterate and prodigal and has to face difficulties at every step in life; also he is not able to get any co-operation from friends or members of the family.

If the mount is not prominent, the person is considered unlucky. His nature becomes irritable and troublesome.

11. The Mount of Dragon's Head: On the palm the area of this mount is situated below the head line, surrounded by the mounts of Moon, Mars and Venus. The fate line passes over this mount while going towards the mount of Saturn.

If the area of the mount of Dragon's Head is prominent and protruded, then the person will certainly be very fortunate and if the fate line is deep and clear while passing over the prominent mount, the person will be a benefactor in his life, genius, religious-minded and will enjoy all worldy comforts. If the fate line is broken on the palm but the mount of Dragon's Head is prominent, the person will grow very wealthy once but he will fall down equally quickly as well. If this mount changes its position and gets in the centre of the palm, then the person faces extremely adverse days in his youth. If the centre of the palm is deep and the fate line proceeds ahead in broken condition, then that person leads the life of a beggar in his youth. If this mount is less protruded, the person will be of restless nature and will lose all wealth with his own hands.

12. The Mount of Dragon's Tail: The place of this mount is a little above the bracelets, dividing the mounts of Venus and Moon and is near the starting point of the fate line. The effec of this planet is more or less like that of the Dragon's Head.

This planet shows its influence from the 5th year to the 20th year of age. If this mount is ordinarily prominent and protruded and the fate line is deep and clear, the person will be fortunate and will be able to enjoy all pleasures in his life time. Such a child has been seen to get rich even though born in a poor family. If this mount is unusually protruded and the fate line is weak, then he has to experience very hard days in his childhood. The financial position of his family gradually gets weaker and weaker and such a child has to face great difficulties in prosecuting his studies. Such a child is also sick in his childhood.

If this mount is undeveloped and fate line is very prominent, yet he cannot mitigate his suffering from poverty in his life. Therefore, a man can advance only when the mount of Dragon's Tail is prominent, and the fate line is clear and prominent, then only the man can get full success in life. It is clear from this that the prominence of Dragon's Tail is very necessary for a person.

In this way, we see that if the mounts on a man's hand are prominent and developed in the correct way, then only a person can rise fully in life and gain complete success.

◆◆

Pairs of Mounts and Signs on Hand

We have studied the mounts on the palm in the previous chapter but it is seen that generally more than one mount is prominent on a palm. In such a case, the combined result of both the mounts affects the person. It is a bit difficult for our readers to reach at such a result. For their facility, I am explaining the results of such pairs of mounts.

1. Jupiter

Jupiter and Saturn	: eminent and fateful.
Jupiter and Sun	: excellent wealth, respect and high post.
Jupiter and Mercury	: interest in astrology and special success in poetry.
Jupiter and Mars	: valour, courage, efficiency in politics, ability to manage war successfully.
Jupiter and Neptune	: high idealist, amassing much wealth.
Jupiter and Harshala	: interest in science, benevolently disposed.
Jupiter and Dragon's Head	: evil genious, want of self-confidence.
Jupiter and Pluto	: good speaker, fertile brain, genius.
Jupiter and Dragon's Tail	: obstacles, difficulties and failures in life.
Jupiter and Moon	: seriousness and influential personality.

Jupiter and Venus	:	attractive personality, special ability to enchant, ability to influence perfectly.

2. Saturn

Saturn and Sun	:	power of reasoning, expansion of scientific ideas.
Saturn and Mercury	:	ability to take decision, benevolent.
Saturn and Venus	:	selfish, amorous, willing to lose all in love matters.
Saturn and Dragon's Head	:	good qualities, amass wealth suddenly in life.
Saturn and Dragon's Tail	:	anxiety for livelihood and mental worries.
Saturn and Neptune	:	foreign travel several times in life.
Saturn and Harshala	:	lover of solitude, expert in many arts.
Saturn and Pluto	:	intelligent, wise and radiant.
Saturn and Moon	:	secret and mysterious personality.
Saturn and Mars	:	quarrelsome nature, destruction of everything when angry.

3. Sun

Sun and Mercury	:	interest in science, ability for international trade.
Sun and Venus	:	working after careful planning.
Sun and Dragon's Head	:	full of anxieties and troubles, difficulties in life.
Sun and Dragon's Tail	:	foreign travels.
Sun and Harshal	:	high fame, rise and intelligent discretion.
Sun and Neptune	:	planning after careful thought.

Sun and Pluto	:	serious and sober personality.
Sun and Moon	:	believer in pomp and artificiality.
Sun and Mars	:	desirous of self-sacrifice.

4. Mercury

Mercury and Venus	:	great attraction for opposite sex, special interest in music.
Mercury and Dragon's Head	:	hot and irritable nature.
Mercury and Dragon's Tail	:	lover of travels, successful human being.
Mercury and Harshala	:	imaginative.
Mercury and Neptune	:	benefactor, well-wisher of the world.
Mercury and Pluto	:	successful international businessman.
Mercury and Moon	:	eminent scientist, rich and farseeing individuality.
Mercury and Mars	:	quick and correct decision-taker.

5. Mount of Venus

Venus and Moon	:	intensity in the desire of love and love for art.
Venus and Dragon's Head	:	sex affairs with women of low class.
Venus and Dragon's Tail	:	development of sympathetic and idealistic feelings.
Venus and Harshala	:	intensity in love matters.
Venus and Neptune	:	high class love for arts and love of humanity.
Venus and Pluto	:	realises struggles of life and able to overcome them.
Venus and Mars	:	expert in music.

6. Moon or Luna

Moon and Mars	:	voyages across the seas.
Moon and Dragon's Head	:	betrayal by friends.
Moon and Dragon's Tail	:	defamation due to love in young age.
Moon and Harshala	:	development of humanism.
Moon and Neptune	:	feeling of ascetism.
Moon and Pluto	:	powerful sexual strength.

7. The Dragon's Head

Dragon's Head and Dragon's Tail	:	struggle for livelihood.
Dragon's Head and Harshala	:	life full of difficulties and troubles.
Dragon's Head and Neptune	:	marriage with a foreign lady.
Dragon's Head and Pluto	:	development of criminal tendencies.

8. The Dragon's Tail

Dragon's Tail and Harshala	:	full of tyrranical ideas.
Dragon's Tail and Neptune	:	absence of wisdom.
Dragon's Tail and Pluto	:	enhanced respect.

9. Harshala

Harshala and Pluto	:	increase in scientific genius.
Harshala and Neptune	:	appointment on high post, foreign travel.

10. Neptune

Neptune and Pluto : sharp and blind sex passion.

SIGNS FOUND ON THE PALM

While studying a palm, signs found on the palm should be carefully observed as these signs are of a great help in prophesying and in providing its results.

The chief kinds of signs found on the palm are:

1. Line
2. Several lines
3. Lines intersecting each other
4. Point
5. Cross
6. Star
7. Square
8. Circle
9. Triangle
10. Net

Now, I am explaining the good and bad results of the signs found on the mounts:

1. The Mount of Jupiter

Single line	: success in all works undertaken.
More than one line	: rise of destiny, interest in new work.
Intersecting lines	: low kind of ideas, struggles in life.
Point	: less respect in society.
Cross	: success in marriage, auspicious ceremonies in the family.
Star	: high desires and their fulfilment.
Square	: beautiful combination of imagination and reality, success in politics and religious work.

Triangle	:	superstitions, inauspicious happenings and losses.
Circle	:	success in every line.
Sign of Jupiter	:	development of qualities found on the mount.
Sign of Saturn	:	success in exorcism.
Sign of Sun	:	interest in fine arts.
Sign of Mercury	:	efficiency in administration.
Sign of Venus	:	love with high family ladies.
Sign of Moon	:	expert in war strategy.

2. The Mount of Saturn

One line	:	rise in luck.
Several lines	:	constant difficulties in life.
Intersecting lines	:	bad luck and anxieties.
Point	:	increased number of unexpected happening.
Cross	:	weakness and impotency.
Star	:	evolution of the desire to murder.
Square	:	safety from calamities.
Circle	:	interest in auspicious work.
Triangle	:	increase in mysterious actions.
Net	:	hard luck.
Sign of Saturn	:	interest in religious, philosophical and exorcist activities.
Sign of Jupiter	:	worldwide fame in philosophy.
Sign of Sun	:	increase in artistic beauty.
Sign of Mercury	:	interest in astrology.
Sign of Venus	:	passionate love towards opposite sex and failure therein.
Sign of Mars	:	judge and love of justice.

3. The Mount of Sun

One line	:	increase in wealth, respect and honour.
Several lines	:	artistic taste, appointment on high post.
Intersecting lines	:	difficulties in service.
Point	:	insult and defeat.
Cross	:	decrease in fame.
Star	:	getting wealth and high post.
Square	:	special respect in society.
Circle	:	foreign travel several times in life.
Triangle	:	high honour in the field of arts.
Net	:	insult.
Sign of Sun	:	worldwide fame, much wealth by means of arts.
Sign of Saturn	:	interest in exorcism.
Sign of Jupiter	:	success in politics.
Sign of Mercury	:	expert conversationalist.
Sign of Venus	:	special bent towards poetry and fine arts.
Sign of Moon	:	success in literary pursuits.
Sign of Mars	:	famous soldier and commander.

4. The Mount of Mercury

One line	:	wealthy and prosperous.
Several lines	:	extraordinary expertise in business.
Intersecting lines	:	successful physician.
Point	:	heavy loss in business.
Cross	:	insolvent.
Star	:	trade with foreign countries.
Square	:	capable of knowing the future.
Circle	:	accidental and unexpected death.

Net	:	defamation.
Spot	:	failure in business.
Sign of Mercury	:	successful trader.
Sign of Jupiter	:	ordinary qualifications of science.
Sign of Saturn	:	frustration in every walk of life.
Sign of Sun	:	evolution of religious side and expertise in astronomy.
Sign of Venus	:	scandalous love in order to obtain wealth.
Sign of Moon	:	tendency to cheat and intrigue.
Sign of Mars	:	success in cheating and deceiving.

5. The Mount of Venus

One line	:	keen sex desire.
Several lines	:	very indulgent.
Intersecting lines	:	failure in love and dishonour.
Point	:	disease of private parts.
Cross	:	failure in love and development of frustration.
Star	:	loss of money on account of beloved.
Square	:	jail term.
Circle	:	injury to body in accident.
Triangle	:	sexual relations with several women in life.
Net	:	sickly body.
Sign of Venus	:	specially indulgent.
Sign of Jupiter	:	flatterer.
Sign of Saturn	:	jealous and unjust feeling of love.
Sign of Sun	:	ideal love.
Sign of Mercury	:	love for money.
Sign of Moon	:	ideas full of sensual pleasures.

Sign of Mars	:	rape on many women several times in life.

6. The Mount of Mars

One line	:	courage.
Several lines	:	tendencies of violence.
Intersecting lines	:	tendency of war and ideas of violence.
Point	:	bodily injury in war.
Cross	:	death in war.
Star	:	appointment on specially high post in military.
Square	:	feeling of too much anger.
Circle	:	clever adept in policies.
Triangle	:	working on pre-plan.
Net	:	suicide.
Sign of Mars	:	development of the tendencies of war.
Sign of Jupiter	:	able to attract women.
Sign of Saturn	:	cruel and cunning nature.
Sign of Sun	:	fond of display.
Sign of Mercury	:	unexpected gain in wealth.
Sign of Venus	:	impatience in love matters.
Sign of Moon	:	insanity.

7. The Mount of Moon

One line	:	development of the feeling of imagination.
Several lines	:	love for beauty.
Intersecting lines	:	anxieties.
Point	:	repeated failures in love.
Cross	:	decreasing respect in society.
Star	:	honour in government.
Square	:	acquiring wealth specially.
Circle	:	death due to drowning.

Triangle	:	poet of countrywide fame.
Net	:	frustration.
Sign of Moon	:	fool.
Sign of Jupiter	:	advancement by force of courage.
Sign of Saturn	:	blind believer and half-mad.
Sign of Sun	:	tendencies for gambling.
Sign of Venus	:	impulse for new ideas.
Sign of Mars	:	insanity.

8. The Dragon's Head-Dragon's Tail

One line	:	courage.
Several lines	:	severe anger.
Intersecting lines	:	want of responsibility.
Point	:	success in every work.
Cross	:	dishonour.
Star	:	special success in the affair of war.
Square	:	honour by government.
Circle	:	very high post in the army.
Triangle	:	acquiring limitless wealth.
Net	:	life of penury.
Sign of Sun	:	weakness.
Sign of Moon	:	insanity.
Sign of Mars	:	robber or murderer.
Sign of Mercury	:	earning money by base deeds.
Sign of Jupiter	:	irreligious.
Sign of Venus	:	sex relations with low class women.
Sign of Saturn	:	notorious deceiver.

9. Harshala

One line	:	special honour.
Several lines	:	foreign travels again and again.

Intersecting lines	: death due to aeroplane accident.
Point	: fame of a high order.
Cross	: obliged to live in a foreign country.
Star	: fame in foreign countries.
Square	: interest in scientific activities.
Circle	: special monetary gain.
Triangle	: taste in engineering works.
Net	: death in accident.
Sign of Sun	: worldwide respect and fame.
Sign of Moon	: special success in life.
Sign of Mars	: appointment to a high post in army.
Sign of Mercury	: import-export trader.
Sign of Jupiter	: composer of religious poems.
Sign of Venus	: high class love.
Sign of Saturn	: successful politician.

10. Neptune

One line	: success in the society.
Several lines	: honour due to performance of social work.
Intersecting lines	: hopelessness in every work.
Point	: lover of justice and fairplay.
Cross	: evolution of the idea of murdering.
Star	: voyages.
Square	: national level honour.
Circle	: mental weakness.
Triangle	: marriage in a foreign country.
Net	: death by drowning.
Sign of Sun	: special success.
Sign of Moon	: gain by trading on a sea coast.

Sign of Mars	:	profit by trading in armaments.
Sign of Mercury	:	international trader.
Sign of Jupiter	:	evolution of a successful social idea.
Sign of Venus	:	sexual intercourse with more than hundred women.
Sign of Saturn	:	impotency.

11. Pluto

One line	:	complete progress in life.
Several lines	:	special honour in the society.
Intersecting lines	:	evolution of the feeling of ascetism.
Point	:	failure in every work.
Cross	:	suicide.
Star	:	interest in religious affairs.
Square	:	foolishness.
Circle	:	interest in auspicious practices.
Triangle	:	success in several arts.
Net	:	unsuccessful life.
Sign of Sun	:	special honour.
Sign of Moon	:	death by drowning.
Sign of Mars	:	fanaticism.
Sign of Mercury	:	special success in trade.
Sign of Jupiter	:	honourable place in the society.
Sign of Venus	:	love for virtue.
Sign of Saturn	:	taste for exorcism.

In brief, I am giving the plus-planets and the minus-planets in the following lines. A person gets the result of the mounts in his life according to the date of his birth. If the mount is a plus, the person is bestowed with the plus points of the mount; if it is minus, the person gets the evils of the mount.

Plus Mounts

Date of Birth	Planet (Plus)
From 20th April to 20th May	Venus
From 21st March to 21 st April	Mars
From 21st Nov. to 30th December	Jupiter
From 21st Dec. to 20th January	Saturn
From 21st July to 20th August	Sun
From 21st May to 20th June	Mercury
From 21st July to 20th August	Moon or Luna

Along with this, I am explaining the minus mounts also. Persons born at this time get the minimum benefits of the mounts of planets.

Minus Mounts

Persons born between the following dates have minus results of the mounts of planets:

Date of Birth	Planet (Minus)
21st September to 20th October	Venus
21st October to 20th November	Mars
19th February to 20th March	Jupiter
21st January to 18th February	Saturn
21st March to 20th April	Sun
21st August to 20th September	Mercury
21st July to 20th August	Moon

In fact, the study of the palm in itself is very difficult but if the lines on it are studied carefully and with perseverance and patience, then one can achieve complete and excellent success in his life.

Lines

The pulsating speed of the life force can be known through the palm and this force combines the lines and mounts in one knot in the palm. As I have said before, no line imprinted on the palm is useless because any line however big or small, thick or thin, is helpful in determining the speed of the life force. Therefore, it is necessary for an expert palmist to make a critical study of each line found on the palm.

The clear and deep long lines on a palm indicates success, while the broken, thin and indistinct lines are a handicap in the life force of an individual. Therefore, the influence of only distinct lines fall on a man's life.

An expert palmist should study both the hands of the person with a microscopic eye. At the same time, he should observe even the tiniest line as each line found on a palm has its own importance and indicates one or the other happenings or facts of life.

The exact time of happenings can also be ascertained by means of lines. The longer the experience, the more correct he will be in fixing the time.

It is necessary to get the correct idea of the lines before the study of the hand. Every man has **7 main lines** and **12 secondary** or **complimentary lines**.

Seven Main Lines:

1. Life line
2. Head line
3. Heart line
4. Line of the Sun or Apollo
5. Fate line
6. Health line
7. Marriage line or Love line.

In addition to these, there are 12 secondary lines. Though these are called secondary lines, yet they have independent significance on a palm and have very great importance in life.

Secondary Lines:

1. Ring of Jupiter
2. Line of Mars
3. Ring of Saturn
4. Ring of Apollo
5. Ring of Venus
6. Ring of Moon or Luna
7. Line of brilliance
8. Journey line
9. Children line
10. Bracelets
11. Casual lines
12. High post lines.

These lines should be studied carefully but it is advisable to know all about the lines before studying them. Chiefly, there are four kinds of lines:

1. Thick Lines: These are such lines which are deep in themselves, distinct and ordinarily wide. Such lines are visible in dim light also.

2. Thin Lines: These lines are thin from the beginning to the end but are distinct. Such lines are said to be more effective.

3. Deep Lines: Such lines generally are thin but at the same time, they are deep and it seems that these appear to have penetrated into the flesh of the palm.

4. Sloping Lines: These are thick in the beginning but they go on getting comparatively thinner as they proceed further.

The following knowledge is also necessary for readers with the knowledge of these lines:

1. Lines should be distinct, beautiful, reddish and clear. There should neither be a sign of any kind nor any island in their path. At the same time, these should not be broken.

2. If the lines on a palm are a little yellowish, then such lines show weak health and defective blood. Such lines also depict frustrative feelings.
3. Reddish lines show the cheerful and healthy psychology of the person. This makes it clear that the person is cheerfully healthy and frank.
4. Black lines on the palm show despondency and weakness.
5. Withered (faint) or weaker lines indicate the future difficulties.
6. If some lines proceed along with a particular line, then this particular line gets special support and it has a special influence.
7. If a secondary line is seen proceeding along with a broken line, then the adverse effect of such broken line is minimised.
8. If any other line than the life line after reaching its end gets divided into two parts, then such a line is considered very auspicious and influential, but, in case the heart line gets parted into two parts at its end, the person meets his death at an early age by heart attack.
9. If any line gets divided into several parts at its end, then this line has opposite effect.
10. If a new line is born which branches off and goes upwards, then the influence of the original line is increased.
11. If a new line is born and branches off from any line and bends downwards or moves downwards, then it has opposite effects on the result of the original line.
12. If any line branches off from the love line and goes upwards, then a beautiful husband is destined. On the other hand, if a line branches off and goes downwards, then the wife of that man dies soon.
13. If a line branches off and goes upwards from the head line, such a person gets special fame.
14. Chained formation of line is considered inauspicious.
15. A person is unsuccessful in love if the marriage line has chained formation.
16. A person gets mad if the head line has chained formation.

17. Zig-zag lines on the palm are not auspicious.
18. Broken line gives only inauspicious results.
19. If a line is very thin and weak, its effects are almost negligible.
20. If an island or a sign is seen in the path of a line, it cannot be considered auspicious.
21. If there is a square in the course of the line, then this line gets support and an auspicious result is obtained from it.
22. If a point is found on a line, then the work connected with the line gets harmed.
23. If a triangle is visible on any line, then the work connected with the line will soon be completed.
24. Oblique slanting lines on a line are considered harmful.
25. If a star is seen on a line, then success is attainable soon.
26. Thick lines show the weakness of a man.
27. Thin lines are competent in giving excellent results in one's life.
28. Sloping lines show the hard work of the person but it does not show the likelihood of excellent results.
29. If a deep line stops in its course or gets weak, then such a line is indicative of accidents.
30. A line is not auspicious if it is thin at some places while thick at others and it should be known that such a person will get cheated several times in his life.
31. Lines should be studied carefully and foretelling should only be done if the signs are found on both the hands of the person.

COMMENCEMENT OF LINES

I have given only a general information about lines in the previous lines of this but we should also know exact place of commencement of these lines.

1. The Life Line: It is called *Jeevan-Rekha* or *Ayu Rekha*. Men call it 'paternal line' or 'age line' also. This line has the greatest importance on a palm. Everything is there if life is there. The effect of all lines will come to an end if life is finished.

The life line commences from under the mount of Jupiter and originates from the side of the palm. The thumb and the index finger, surrounding the mount of Venus, ultimately end at the bracelets.

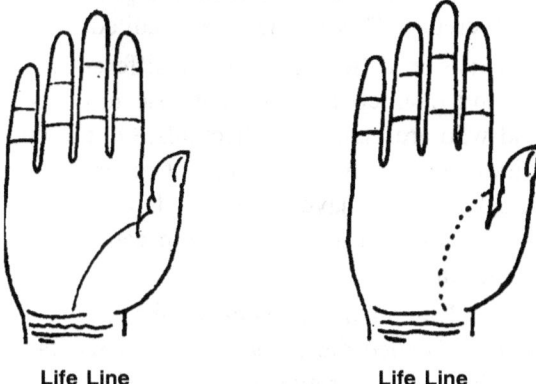

Life Line   **Life Line**

This line is seen at this very place in the hands of all living beings. A person's age, health, sickness, all can be known from this line.

This line is not alike in the palms of all persons. This line is deep and long in some hands while some lines make the mount of Venus of the person very narrow. In some persons' palms, this line gets almost broken up on reaching near the mount of Venus. Such persons are certainly shortlived and they die due to accidents.

This line can ordinarily show all about a person's whole life.

2. The Head Line: This line is called *Mastishk Rekha* in Hindi. This line starts from near the mount of Jupiter or from above it. In majority of the cases, I have seen the head line and the life line

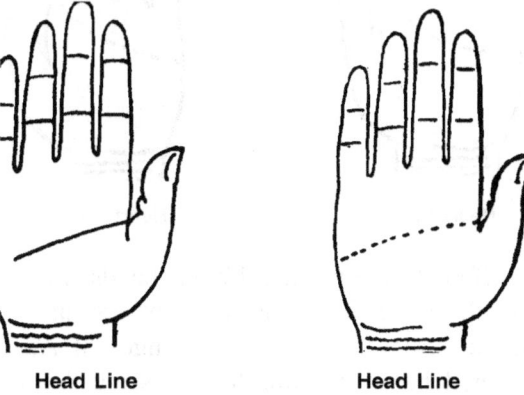

Head Line   **Head Line**

originating from one and the same place. In some hands, the source of these lines is not found to be the same but it is quite close to one another. This line divides the palm into two parts, separates the areas of the Dragon's Head and the Harshala and goes under the area of the mount of Mercury. This whole line is called the 'Head Line'.

This line exists in different ways on different hands. This line is long, deep and distinct in persons whose mind is sharp, fertile and active and who are mainly intellectuals. On the other hand, this line is faint, indistinct or appears broken at several places in persons who are manual workers, have weak minds or earn their living by sheer labour. The study of a person's brain can be completely done by means of this line.

3. The Heart Line: This line is called the 'Heart line' in English while in Hindi it is called the *Vichar Rekha*. This starts from under the mount of Mercury, separating the areas of the Mercury and the Harshala, reaching under the index finger and the mount of Jupiter. Ordinarily, this line is found in the hands of all persons because this line has a direct relationship with the heart but I have seen a complete absence of this line in some robbers and cruel persons. Persons, in whose hands this line is weak, are generally found to be inhuman and merciless.

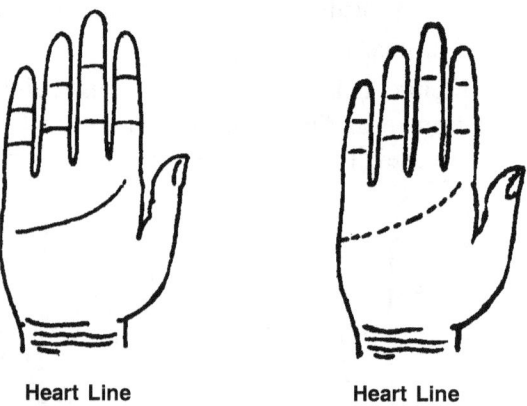

Heart Line   Heart Line

It is of different lengths in different hands. In some hands, it prolongs upto the index finger, in some others, upto the finger of Saturn, while in still others, upto the finger of Apollo. In some others, however, I have seen this line crossing the area of Jupiter and reaching the other end of the palm but such long line is seen in a very few persons.

4. The Line of Apollo or Sun : It is also called the 'Apollo line' or the 'Sun line' or the 'Line of Success'. In Hindi, it is known as *Surya Rekha, Ravi Rekha* or *Pratibha Rekha*. The source of this line has been seen at different places in different hands but one thing is common to all hands and this is that this line invariably finishes at the mount of Sun. I have seen this line commencing from 30 different places. Therefore, a line which terminates at the mount of Sun can be accepted to be the Apollo line.

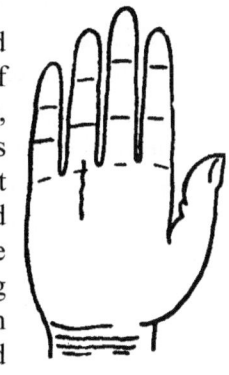

Apollo Line

5. The Fate Line : It is called the 'Fate Line' in English. In Hindi, it is known as *Bhagya Rekha*.

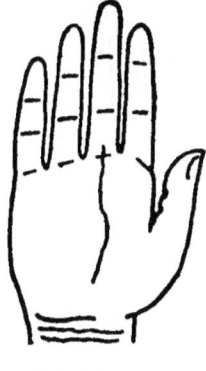 

Fate Line   **Fate Line**

This line is not visible in all the hands. At the same time, this line commences at different places but one thing should be clearly understood that only that line can be called the 'Fate Line' which terminates at the mount of Saturn. Till this line does not reach this mount, it is not proper to call it a fate line.

In some hands this line reaches the mount of Mercury but in fact this line is some other line than the fate line. This line develops from below the palm towards the upper side. In some hands, this line commences from the mount of Venus, while in some others, it starts from the bracelets and appears to rise upwards. In some hands this line commences from near the mount of Sun and reaches the mount of Saturn. Therefore, as I have said that this line originates from different places hence, its source of commencement should be found out from the place of its termination.

This line is not found on the hands of more than 50% of the people of the world.

6. The Health Line: This line is called the *Swasthya Rekha* in Hindi. This line relates to health but there is no fixed place of its source. This line can commence from the mount of Mars or from Life Line or from the centre of the palm or from any other place but it should be remembered that this line invariably terminates at the mount of Mercury and the line which reaches the mount of Mercury can really be called the 'Health Line'. In some hands, it is very thick, while in others it is found thinner than hair. This line should be studied with great care. Health, sickness etc. are studied with its help.

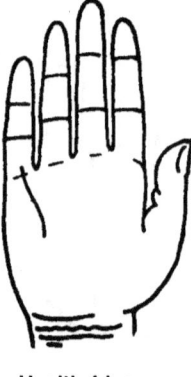   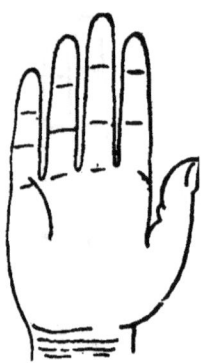

Health Line   **Health Line**

7. The Marriage Line: In English it is called the 'Love Line' or the 'Marriage Line'. It is situated on the mount of Mercury. The line which is seen coming from the outside of the palm towards the inside of the palm on the mount of Mercury is called the marriage line. In some hands, there are 3 or 4 such lines but from this, it should not be concluded that the man will marry 3 or 4 women. Though it does show that he will surely have sex relationship with 3 or 4 women. The line, which is deep and distinct out of these 3 or 4 lines, is called the 'Marriage Line'.

It has also been observed several times that a person remains life-long bachelor inspite of the presence of the marriage line in his hand. The reason for this is that if there is any kind of cross in the marriage line, it can be concluded that his engagement will be broken. He won't get married in his lifetime. If there are some small signs on any line on the side of the marriage line, then the man will have several illegal affairs.

I have explained all main lines above. Now I am going to describe the 'supporting lines'.

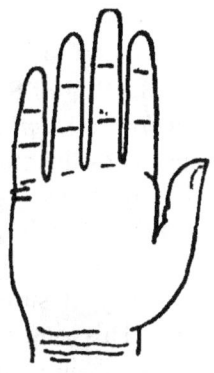
Marriage Line

1. Ring of Jupiter: It is called the 'Ring of Jupiter'. English and in Hindi, it is known as *Guru Mudra* or *Guru Valaya* also. It makes a half moon sign under the index finger on the mount of Jupiter and covers its whole area which looks like a ring. This is called 'Ring of Jupiter'.

2. Line of Mars: This line commences from the base of the life line near the thumb, passes over the area of Mars and goes towards the mount of Venus and the line of Mars, but its place of commencement is not sure. On some persons' hands, it is seen in the middle of the life line while in others, it moves side by side with the life line. It begins to move further away from the life line when it proceeds towards the mount of Venus.

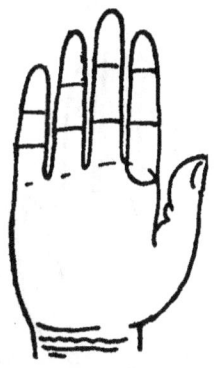
Ring of Jupiter

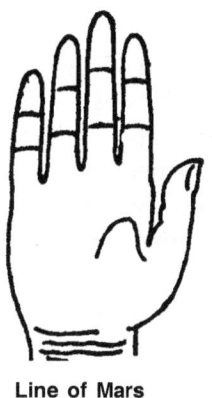
Line of Mars

Line of Mars

In the palm, the presence of this line is considered to be very auspicious.

3. Ring of Saturn: In Hindi, it is called *Shani Mudra* or *Shani Rekha* or *Shani Valaya*. This line surrounds the mount of Saturn in the base finger of Saturn. Its one end lies between the finger of Saturn and the index finger and the other end lies between the finger of Saturn and the finger of Apollo. In this way, it surrounds the mount of Saturn in a ring. This ring wields a great significance in the study of the palm.

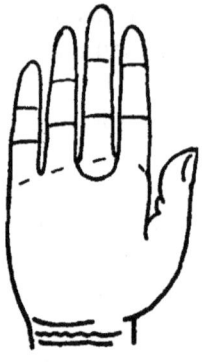

Ring of Saturn

Ring of Sun

4. Ring of Sun: In Hindi, it is called *Surya Mudra* or *Surya Valaya*. It surrounds the mount of Sun like a ring. The one end of this ring lies between the finger of Saturn and the finger of Sun and the other end lies between the finger of Sun and the little finger. The shape of this ring remains the same in every hand.

5. Girdle of Venus: In English, it is called the 'Girdle of Venus' and in Sanskrit, *Bhrigu Rekha*, *Sutra Rekha* or *Sutra Valaya*. It commences between the index finger and the finger of Saturn and ends between the finger of Apollo and the little finger. In this way, it encircles both the mounts of the Saturn and Sun. In some hands, this ring is formed by double lines. Though its name is girdle of Venus but it has no connection with the mount of Venus. This ring is said to be of great importance in a person's hand.

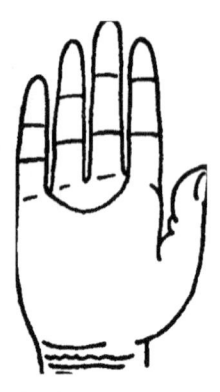

Girdle of Venus

6. The Moon Line: It is a line in the shape of a bow. It commences from the area of the Moon, passes over the Neptune and Harshal areas and ends after reaching the mount of Mercury. This line is seen on very few hands.

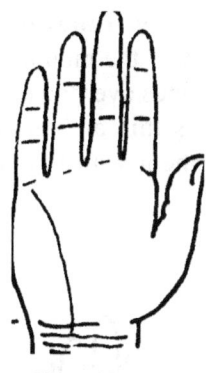

Moon Line

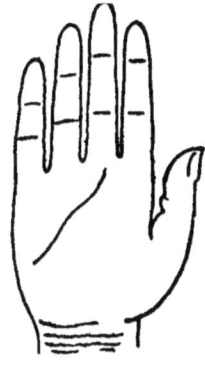

Line of Influence

7. Line of Influence: It is called the 'Line of Influence' in English. It enhances the influence of any line with which it is found. This line passes over the areas of the Moon and Neptune and reaches the Fate line. In some persons' hands it is dual while in some other hands it is treble. Its origin can be observed from the mount of Venus also but this kind of origin has been observed in very few hands.

8. Travelling Line: It denotes travel of any kind—air travel, sea travel or travel on foot. If seen critically, it can be known that there are different signs on this line from which the kind of travel can be known. It passes over the line of Moon or is seen proceeding from the area of Venus towards the area of Mars and is seen crossing the area of Dragon's Head, moving towards the mount of Moon. Such lines are both thick and thin.

Travelling Line

9. Lines of Children: These lines are seen near the mount of Mercury in the form of vertical lines over the marriage line. In fact, these lines are as thin as hair and it is not possible to decipher them with the naked eye.

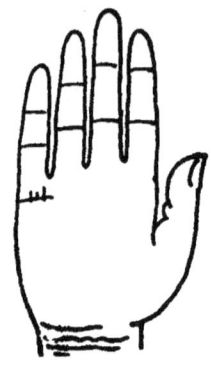

Lines of Children

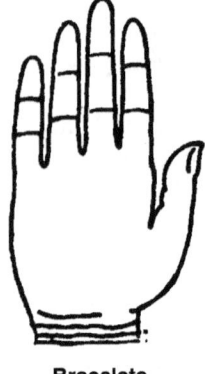

Bracelets

10. Bracelets: These lines are found on the wrist and they are different in number on different hands. In some hands one, in others, two or three or even four wrist lines are seen.

11. Casual Lines : These lines are formed from time to time and show the good and bad times. These lines are not permanent but these disappear when their momentary influence is over. These lines can be formed at any place on the palm and disappear after having been formed.

12. High Post Line : This line commences

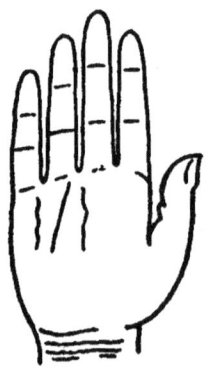

Casual Lines

from the wrist and is seen proceeding towards the area of the Dragon's Tail. If this line is deep and distinct, the person will certainly attain some high post.

I have given a brief introduction of the main and supporting lines above. Now, I am explaining some more details in connection with these lines in the following pages.

◆◆

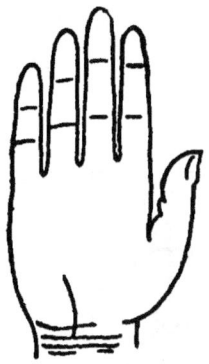

High Post Line

The Life Line

The life line is the only such line which is found on the hands of every person. It should be understood that the person has practically no individuality if this line is not seen in his hand and the life energy in him has altogether vanished. Such a person can meet death at anytime. Several times, the line of Mars supports this line, sometimes the line of Venus is also seen supporting it but if this line is faultless and clear, then only it is considered auspicious for a person.

The age of a person can be known from this line and it can also be known from this line which accidents will take place and at what time in a person's life. Also the time of death and its cause can be known from it.

This line commences from under the mount of Jupiter but several times it is seen starting from above this mount. It is very essential to know about this line that the bigger the area it carves out of the mount of Venus, the more auspicious it is considered. It makes the mount of Venus very narrow several times. If such a thing is seen on the palm, it should be understood that the person's rise in life will be difficult, and in addition to that there will be deficiency of worldy pleasures like love, dalliance and happiness. The person will have very short age if the line passes near the thumb.

The deeper, distinct and unbroken the life line is, the more auspicious it is considered. Such a person will enjoy excellent health, there will be development of feelings of love, affection and beauty in his heart but if this line is broken and torn or indistinct, the person's life will be full of troubles and accidents and he will be emotionless. Such persons are short-tempered, irritable and get angry on the slightest pretext.

If the life line and head line join completely under the mount of Jupiter, then it is considered auspicious. Such a person is hardworking, alert and works according to a planned scheme. But in case both these lines commence at different places, the person has different ideas and works in his own way. But if all the three lines i.e. the life line, the head line and the heart line commence from the same point, this indicates misfortune and such a person is surely murdered.

If zig-zag lines are visible on the life line, the person has weak health. The person is an asthma patient if a triangle is formed between the heart line and the life line.

A person has too many desires, sentiments and ambitions and tries his level best to get them fulfilled if a thin line branches off from life line and is seen proceeding towards the mount of Jupiter. If several lines are seen commencing from this line, the person is hardworking and energetic and makes his own future with his own labour.

If supporting lines are proceeding side by side with the life line then such a person works after careful thought, is a wise planner, clever and ambitious. Nothing is impossible for such a person in life.

If the life line comes to an abrupt end all of a sudden then it is indicative of an unexpected death. If any supporting line branches off from the life line and proceeds towards the mount of Moon, then such a person becomes insane in his old age. If the line of Saturn joins this line then the person is genius and brilliant.

A person dies suddenly if any kind of point of cross is visible at the end of the life line. A person will surely suffer from tuberculosis in his old age if the life line gets divided into several parts at its end.

Some other facts are being explained in this connection :

1. Small line : short age.
2. Yellow and wide line : sickness and controversial character.
3. Red line : feeling of violence.
4. Thin line : unexpected death.
5. Chained line : delicate body.
6. Broken line : sickness.
7. Ladder-like line : sickness throughout life.
8. Commencing from under the mount of Jupiter : grand success.

9. In close contact with the Head line : life full of wisdom.
10. Junction of Head and Heart and Life lines : unfortunate personality.
11. In-set deep line : uncourteous behaviour.
12. Star near the Health and Head lines : childlessness.
13. Distinct line : life full of justice.
14. Cluster of branches at the point of origin : unsettled life.
15. Branches between the lines : life full of tuberculosis.
16. Branches at the terminal point : old age full of difficulties.
17. Division in two at the end : death in poverty.
18. Network at the end : death after heavy financial loss.
19. Supporting line rising above the main line : unexpected gain of wealth.
20. Black spot on the line : beginning of sickness.
21. Supporting lines proceeding downwards : loss of health and wealth.
22. Breaking of lines on its path : financial loss.
23. Intersecting lines at several places : permanent sickness.
24. Square on the line : murder.
25. Cross in the beginning : loss of limbs in accident.
26. Cross at the end of the line : unsuccessful old age.
27. Cross cutting the life line : mental weakness.
28. Island in the beginning of the line : interest in the science of charms.
29. Island in the middle of the line : body weakness.

30. Zig-zag life line and island over it : sick life.
31. Lines proceeding outside the hand from the life line : anxieties and troubles.
32. Line proceeding from life line to the mount of Jupiter : success at every step.
33. Lines proceeding towards the mount of Saturn : accident with animal and death.
34. Lines proceeding towards the mount of Apollo : fame and honour.
35. Lines proceeding towards the mount of Mercury : special success in international trade.
36. Lines proceeding towards the mount of Moon : too much power.
37. Lines going towards the low mount of Mars : suicide in anger.
38. Lines proceeding towards the mount of Mars : slander in young age due to love affair.
39. Lines proceeding towards the inside of the mount of Venus : lost love.
40. Line cutting the life line at several places : failure in family life.
41. Line cutting the life line and reaching head line : complete failure in business.
42. Line proceeding towards head line after cutting life line : insanity.
43. Line proceeding towards heart line after cutting the life line : heart trouble.
44. Line cutting the life line and the heart line : failure in love affairs.

45. Island at the end of the : troublesome married life.
    line proceeding towards the
    heart line.
46. Line cutting the life line : downfall in the society.
    and the Sun line
47. Sign of Star on the : domestic quarrels.
    mount of Venus and
    life line
48. Star sign on the life line : troublesome domestic quarrel.
    and the Sun line
49. Signs on the Head line, : diseased life.
    Heart line and the life line
50. Triangle on the fate line : financial loss.
    and the life line
51. Triangle on the Sun line : criminal life.
    and life line

◆◆

Head Line

Life and the brain are closely connected with one another as life becomes almost useless without wisdom or intelligence. Fame, honour, respect are all obtained by intelligence. So, the importance of the life line and the head line are almost equal in life.

According to the learned palmists, it is very necessary for the head line to be strong, firm and distinct on the palm—otherwise the whole life is spoiled if the head line is even slightly defective.

Head line has no fixed source. It commences from different places. Chiefly, it originates from the following places:

1. It commences from the starting point of the life line and reaches the other side of the palm after cutting the life line itself.
2. It ends in the centre of the palm after commencing from near the source of the life line.
3. It changes its course after proceeding side by side with the life line for quite a long distance.
4. It reaches the other end commencing from near the life line and divides the palm into two parts.
5. The head line and the heart line appear to proceed almost merged into one another. But there are also other sources of the head line.

If the head line is seen similar to no. 1, it is not considered favourable because such a line proceeds after cutting the life line and such a sign indicates accident in a person's life. Such a person remains sick and weak in life. He gets angry on the slightest pretext and not being prudent does something to harm himself. Number of friends is less in the life of such a person and even the friends cheat at the time of need.

The second type of head line which originates from the origin of the life line and ends in the middle of the palm, indicates that the person will surely reach a position of importance in life. There is a perfect harmony in the thoughts and actions in the life of such a person and he is able to take quick decisions and recognise the opportunities when the occasion comes. Such a person has sharp intelligence and is capable of reaching the very bottom of the thing. He can attain complete success in life through travelling.

A person having the source of the third kind of head line (which changes its course after proceeding with the life line) on his palm, is full of self-confidence and is very clever and efficient in getting its work done. He has more than one source of income. Though, at times, he does feel an inferiority complex but still he succeeds in life by dint of his energy and industry.

A person having the source of head line of the fourth kind on his palm is destined to go on foreign travels several times in his life. At the same time, he gains much wealth by carrying on trade in foreign countries. Such a person is considered fully successful from the materialistic point of view.

A person having the source of head line of the fifth kind on his palm is harsh, cruel and has no feelings and is emotionless. In a way, he has no heart worth the name. Such sources are often seen on the palms of most of the criminals. If on such a palm only the head line is visible and the heart line is not visible or the head and heart lines have got mixed up on the palm or have intertwined between themselves, then such a person commits several murders in his life and becomes a ferocious dacoit.

In fact, a palmist should pay special attention to the source of the head line while studying a hand and make up his mind after observing its source as the source of the head line makes clear several new facts.

Other facts in connection with the head line are being explained in the following lines:

1. If any thin line is proceeding from the head line towards the mount of Jupiter then such a person is wise and acts according to plans.
2. If such a line is straight, distinct and faultless, then such a person will take immediate decisions, has an active mind and is wise.
3. If the sources of the head line and life line are at different places, then such a person is of independent nature. He

acts according to his own will and does not work under the influence or force of anyone else.

4. If there are different sources of the head line and the life line in a woman's hand, then such a woman will be a flirt.
5. If a line branches off from the head line and reaches the end of the mount of Jupiter, then such a person will be a noted writer or artist of the country. He will be able to live a decent and grand life.
6. A person has very great love for money if the head line passes through the middle of the palm and bends downwards. He is desirous of living a luxurious life but he is not able to fulfil them because of the state of affairs.
7. A person will have affairs with several women other than his own wife if the head line proceeds further and touches the heart line but he gets defamed in life because of it.
8. A person murders his own wife or mistress in anger if the head line proceeds intertwined with the heart line.
9. If the head line is specially leaning towards any mount, the attributes of such a mount gets increased. If it leans towards the mount of Jupiter, then the person will be the best writer.
10. A person can get a very high post if this line is seen leaning towards the mount of Sun.
11. A person becomes a philosopher or thinker if this line goes towards the mount of Saturn.
12. A person becomes a successful trader and thereby earns enormous wealth if the head line seems to lean towards the mount of Mercury.
13. A person is of uncertain mind, says something else and does quite another thing if the head line proceeds in a zig-zag course.
14. A person surely becomes a poet and undertakes sea voyages several times in his life if the head line is seen proceeding towards the mount of the Moon.
15. A person remains life-long poor, sorrowful and unemployed if the head line reaches the wrist after passing over the mount of Moon.

16. A person certainly gets insane in old age if the sign of a cross is found at the point where the head line terminates.
17. A person remains busy in collecting money in various ways if the head line divides into two parts near its end. Such a person can easily get wealth, fame, respect, rank and honour in life.
18. A person surely commits suicide if this line terminates on reaching the wrist and there is sign of cross beyond it.
19. A person remains unsuccessful in life if the head line terminates at the mount of Mars.
20. A person remains unsuccessful in life and is called insane if the head line proceeds towards the mount of Saturn and there is cross sign at the end.
21. A person will get very sick at the age the head line cuts the heart line.
22. A person is called very lucky if there is double head line on the palm, i.e., the subsidiary line also moves side by side with the head line.
23. A person can surely attain complete success in diplomacy if the double head line is straight, distinct and plain.
24. A person is of unbalanced mind if the head line gets broken during its course.
25. A person may get grievously injured during childhood if the head line gets broken under the mount of Jupiter. Similarly, if it breaks below the mount of Saturn, then the person gets injury from a weapon.
26. A person has to face much defame in service if the head line abruptly ends under the mount of Sun. The person becomes insolvent if such a line breaks under the mount of Mercury.
27. A person suffers from mental illness in life if the head line is chained.
28. A person becomes insane if there is some kind of island on the head line under the mount of Jupiter.
29. A person will have to go to the lunatic asylum in the 24th year of his life if there is an island on the head line under the mount of Saturn.

30. A person remains unsuccessful in life in every way if an island is seen on the head line under the mount of the Sun.
31. A person gets killed due to explosion if an island is formed on the head line under the mount of Mercury.
32. If the head line has been cut in its course, then the person is of unbalanced mind.
33. If small fine lines are seen near the head line, the person is of unsteady mind.
34. If the head line is seen proceeding towards the mount of Venus after a winding course, the person is very popular among women.
35. If white point is visible on the head line, the person can attain complete success in life.
36. If black spots or points are seen on the head line, the person is of defective mind.
37. If there is a sign of cross on this line, the person can die from an accident.
38. If there is a sign of star on this line, the person gets grievously injured in life.
39. If there is a sign of circle on this line, the person is not farsighted and is foolish.
40. If there is sign of a triangle on this line, the person has to bear huge loss.
41. If one has long fingers and the head line also is straight and distinct, the person is wise and farsighted.
42. If fingers are small but the head line is distinct, the person cannot attain complete success in life.
43. If all the mounts are firm and the head line also is straight and distinct, the person surely can attain success in life with his own efforts.
44. If the fingers on the hand are pointed and the head line is straight, the person will be learned.
45. If there is a sign of a triangle at the end of the heart line and the life line it is considered very auspicious.
46. If the head line is seen proceeding across the whole length and breadth of the palm, the person has very sharp memory and is considered very promising in life.

47. If the head line has rings, the person will always suffer from sickness of the head.
48. If the thumb is small and the head line is faint, the person gets insolvent by his own folly.
49. If the mount of Mercury is developed but the head line is weak, the person has to bear very great treachery.
50. If the palm is wide and the mount of Sun is weak but the head line is distinct, the person cannot attain success in life.
51. Thin heart line depicts mental weakness of a person.
52. If there are several small islands on the head line, the person dies due to delirium.
53. If the head line is zig-zag, the person is very narrow-minded.
54. If the heart line is weak and the head line is distinct, the person suffers from tuberculosis in life.
55. If the life line has its source above and proceeds onwards and there are several small lines, the person is very powerful.
56. If there is a rectangle at the end of this line, the person can attain success in foreign countries.
57. If the mounts of Jupiter and Mars are clear and the head line is distinct, the person has extraordinary self-confidence and has a very strong willpower.
58. If the head line passes near the thumb, the person has very short span of life.
59. If this line is broken at several places as it proceeds towards the heart line, the person suffers from epilepsy in his life.
60. If this line proceeds side by side with the life line, the person meets his death due to treachery in love affairs.
61. If this line ends at the mount of Moon, the person is a famous exorcist.
62. If this line is like a net, the person is an excellent speaker.
63. If this line proceeds onwards in zig-zag manner, the person loses all his property in gambling.
64. If this line ends in the centre of the palm, the person is insane.
65. If this line turns back after proceeding for some distance, the person meets with an unpleasant end in love affair.

66. If this line ends near the fate line, the person dies before reaching the age of 25 years.
67. If the end of this line is towards the mount of Mercury, the person does things in an orderly manner. If the end is on the mount of Mars, the person remains worried with mental troubles.
68. If the line is divided into small parts, the person is very proud.
69. If the line breaks under the area of the Sun, the person gets killed by the attack of a wild animal.
70. If the head line and the life line join and make an acute angle, the person reaches a very high post in government service.
71. If this line proceeds side by side with the life line towards the heart line, the person is found to be blind.
72. If there is a cross sign at the end of the head line and the health line, the person will have to suffer from brain diseases.
73. If both the head line and the heart line are broken, the person cannot get happiness of family life.
74. If this line meets the heart line in the centre of the palm, the person is haunted with fear of armed attack in life.
75. If both the health line and the head line are zig-zag, the person has very weak health.
76. If any other line cuts the head line, the person has weak mind.
77. If the head line is broken and there are other lines also, the person remains a lunatic in life.
78. If any line comes out of the mount of Venus and cuts the head line, the family life of the person is spoiled.
79. If any branch line comes out of the head line and proceeds towards the mount of Venus, the person's love affairs remain a life-long secret.
80. If any branch line comes out of this line and proceeds towards the mount of Jupiter, the person becomes a provision merchant.

81. If any secondary line branches off from this line and proceeds towards the mount of Saturn, the person is highly religious in life.
82. If any secondary line branches off from this line and proceeds towards the mount of Sun, the person gets unexpected wealth.
83. If any secondary line branches off and goes towards the mount of Mercury, the person certainly is the master of lakhs of rupees.
84. If there is a cluster of lines at the end of this line, the person is clever, liar and crafty.
85. If there are white spots under the mount of Saturn on this line, the person gets financial success in life.
86. If there are white spots on this line under the mount of Sun, the person gets national honour.
87. If there are white spots on this line under the mount of Mercury, the person will be a multi-millionaire.
88. If the mount of Mars is powerful and there is a triangle at the end of this line, the person surely commits a murder in his life.
89. If there is a red spot anywhere on this line, the person meets his death with injury on the head.
90. If there is any blue spot on this line, the person is a criminal by nature.
91. If this line reaches the root of the index finger, the person remains unsuccessful in life.
92. If this line rides over the finger of Saturn, the person dies from drowning.
93. If this line reaches the end of the finger of Apollo, the person is a famous exorcist.
94. If this line over-rides the finger of Mercury, the person dies under delirious condition.
95. If this line is free from all defects, the person has magnetic attraction.

In fact, the head line has great importance in the palm and if this line is not carefully studied, the foretelling becomes very difficult. Therefore, it is necessary for a palmist to study the head line very carefully and come to a sure conclusion before prophesying, so that he can become famous in his life.

The Heart Line

There is almost equal importance of the heart line on the palm like that of the life line and head line. Therefore, it is necessary for learned palmists to study the heart line carefully.

A person really becomes successful in life and gets complete fame and respect in society if the heart line on his palm is clear, distinct, faultless and reddish. Such persons realise their responsibilities towards the society and go ahead keeping in view the qualities of human beings.

If such a line is indistinct, weak, broken or cut at places, however rich he may be, he cannot be called a human being in the true sense of the word. Because such a person will be selfish, guilty and sinful at heart. Such a person should not be trusted ordinarily.

The heart line originates on a palm under the finger of Mercury. It starts from under the mount of Mercury, crosses the areas of the Sun and Saturn and goes upto the mount of Jupiter. But it is not like this on all hands. Generally this line is one which starts from under the mount of Mercury passing under the Sun and Saturn and terminates at the mount of Jupiter but it is not alike on all hands.

Generally, this line is found in the five following situations:
1. The first kind of head line is one which starts from under the mount of Mercury, passing under the mounts of Sun and Saturn and terminates at the mount of Jupiter.
2. In the hands of some persons, this line starts from under the mount of Mercury, passes under the mounts of Sun, Saturn and Jupiter and reaches the other end of the palm.
3. In some hands, this line starts from under the mount of Mercury and comes to an end under the mount of Sun.
4. In a few hands, this line starts from under the mount of Mercury and comes to an end under the mount of Saturn.

5. In the hands of some persons, this line start from under the mount of Mercury and terminates between the index finger and the finger of Saturn.

The study of the above five kinds results in different conclusions. A person's wishes, his behaviour, his aspirations, his mental activity and internal secret facts can be known by means of this line.

Now I will describe each kind in brief.

First Kind

A person having this kind of heart line is said to have the best. In correct perspective, this line at its end separates the mount of Saturn and Jupiter. Such persons are helpers of others, impartial, independent thinkers and work patiently in love matters. There is no indiscipline or immaturity seen in their lives. Such persons are true to their words and are capable of fulfilling things they promise.

Such a person is not of low standard and gives the highest importance to his wife. It is true that he has mistresses in his life but he does not give more than necessary attention to them. Such a person is pious, religious and honest. Neither does he gets cheated nor does he try to cheat others. He is kind-hearted and his life can be regarded as an ideal life. Such persons get fame, honour, high post and respect in their lives with their own efforts.

Second Kind

In this kind, the heart line originates from under the mount of Mercury and does not terminate between the index finger and the finger of Saturn but near the palm after passing under the mount of Jupiter. This kind of line is seen on the hands of very few persons but if they have this line, they are too much ambitious in their lives and succeed in making their lives happy by their own efforts.

In fact, such persons are very hardworking and they always keep their aim in their front. They don't take rest in life till they have fulfilled their aims.

The fact to be considered about this line is that the point of this line should be carefully studied. If this line is leaning downwards near the point of termination, the person is not able to get his desires fulfilled in his life but in case the line is seen to be going upwards, then the person is able to achieve his aims and all that he thought of is completed. Such a person is called lucky in his life from the point of view of fame, respect, post and honour.

Third Kind

This kind of line starts from under the mount of Mercury and ends under the mount of Sun. Such a person is not far-sighted and is biased. He has a weak heart. He gets irritated on trivial matters and is short-tempered. In fact, such persons are unkind. They don't help persons in trouble. On the contrary, they consider themselves fortunate in defaming them. Such a person cannot be called successful from ordinary points of view.

Such persons remain afflicted with heart troubles in old age and they die of heart attacks.

Fourth Kind

In some persons' palms, this line originates from under the mount of Mercury and terminates under the mount of Saturn. Such persons have love affairs with several women and cheat nearly everyone of them. Cheating and craftiness is always present in their lives. In truth, such persons cannot be fully relied upon.

Their love is not sincere but a means to satisfy their carnal desires. Selfishness is uppermost in their minds and they are clever in cheating others. They believe in false propaganda, false pomp and show and ostentations. At first, people believe in them but afterwards, they begin to despise them. They do not even cast their eyes towards those who help them once their work is done. They don't get any respect or honour in society.

Such persons can be cruel, dacoits and oppressors.

Fifth Kind

Persons on whose hands this type of heart line is seen are self-centred and almost remain lost in their ownselves. Though such persons are very industrious and proceed successfully towards their aim, yet they can't succeed even after repeated efforts. They get tired in the middle of their age.

These persons have fertile brains and commence their work in a planned and orderly manner, but their enthusiasm gets cooled off half-way in the completion of the work which they began with much zeal. Such persons get irritated and after meeting repeated failures in life they become suspicious by nature. It becomes their nature to suspect anyone who comes in their contact. Gradually, they get cut off from friends and acquaintees and frustration overpowers them. Like this later on they find themselves without any helpers and depend upon others.

In the following pages, I am elucidating facts about the heart line with the help of which correct results can be found out.

1. The particular mount under which the heart line reaches will automatically acquire the special qualities of the mount. For example, if the heart line terminates at the mount of Sun situated at the root of the finger of Sun by going under it, then the qualities connected with the Sun, such as, fame, honour, being renowned, etc. will automatically be attributed to this.
2. If the heart line leans towards the head line then the mind gets fully developed corresponding to the age of the point where it begins to lean.
3. If this line proceeding ahead meets the head line completely then the person does not think with his own mind; on the contrary, he works according to what others ask him and thus sacrifices his all in carrying out their orders.
4. If the head line cuts the heart line after moving forward, the mind gets completely perplexed and the person does not remain fully capable of taking decisions himself.
5. If any thin line meets the heart line, then the qualities of that mount from which the line comes have special influence on his heart.
6. A person remains worried with mental trouble throughout his life if thin small lines proceed from the heart line towards the head line.
7. If the heart line is broken at several places, the person falls a victim to heart attack.
8. A person is not able to get special respect in the society and his social life is broken in a way if there is an island on the heart line on the palm.

9. The longer the heart line and the farther it is away from the mount of Jupiter, the more favourable it is considered.
10. If the heart line gets broken in its course and proceeds again, the person gets death-like troubles at that time of life.
11. A person gets complete love and affection from everybody if the heart line is long, distinct and beautiful.
12. A person can become a victim of his blind faith for somebody if the heart line reaches near the palm.
13. A person is constantly full of frustration in life if the heart line is broken at several places.
14. A person loves people on high level but he gets hopelessness in his life if there is another heart line on the palm.
15. If there is a star sign at the end of the heart line, the person meets his death due to a sudden accident.
16. If the heart line moves forward surrounding the mount of Jupiter, the person has very much hatred for all.
17. A person remains sick throughout his life if there is star sign on the heart line.
18. A person gets repeatedly cheated if this line ends at the mount of Apollo.
19. A person is very lascivious if this line ends at the mount of Saturn.
20. A person has to pass his youth in a lunatic asylum if this line goes under the mount of Jupiter and forms a trident.
21. A person dies in young age if the sign of cross is found on the heart line and head line under the mount of Saturn.
22. The greater the length of the heart line than the head line and more distinct and reddish, the more effective it is considered. Such a person gets international honour.
23. Double heart line is helpful in obtaining a very high position.
24. A person does dangerous works in life if the mount of Mars is prominent and the heart line is clear.
25. A person is of low category if the fingers are square in shape and the heart line leans towards the head line as it moves forward.
26. A very small heart line indicates the unluckiness of a person.

27. If the heart line is reddish more than necessary, the person is very violent.
28. If the line is yellowish, the person constantly suffers from heart diseases.
29. If the heart line is very wide, the person remains weak in health throughout his life.
30. If this line is very thin and long, the person is surely a murderer without fail.
31. If the heart line reaches the end of the palm and is very weak in itself, the person will be childless.
32. If the heart line is chain-like, such persons cannot be relied upon. They are clever liars.
33. If this line is chained and ends near the mount of Saturn, the person hates the opposite sex.
34. If the heart line becomes like a chain on the mount of Saturn in the palm of a woman, she is an unchaste woman.
35. If this line gets broken into several pieces near the mount of Sun, the person is weak.
36. A person's married life is troublesome if this line is broken under the mount of Mercury.
37. If a line brances off from the heart line and goes towards the mount of Mars, then the person will be hard-hearted and cruel by nature.
38. Black spots on the heart line are a source of hindrance in marriage matters of a person.
39. If there are white spots on the heart line, the person's married life is ideal.
40. If there is a triangle on the heart line, the person gets worldwide fame.
41. If the heart line bends towards the mount of Mars after reaching the mount of Jupiter, then the person is a fool.
42. If this line ends anywhere along with a square, the person is fickle-minded.
43. A person meets with several accidents in his life if this line meets the head line under the mount of Saturn.

44. If the heart line meets the head line under the mount of Mercury, then the person dies in his youth.
45. If this line leans downwards and proceeds towards the mount of Moon or any line meets it after branching off from the mount of Moon, the person attains unexpected success in life.
46. If some intersecting lines cut the heart line at several places, the person will suffer from several kinds of sicknesses in life.
47. If any supplementary line branches off from the heart line and proceeds towards the head line and joins it, the person has more than necessary capability to love.
48. If any supplementary line branches off from the heart line and proceeds towards the mount of Saturn, the person will meet with failure in love affair.
49. If any subsidiary line branches off from the fate line and touches the heart line, the person's family life is full of worries.
50. If any subsidiary line branches off from the mount of Venus and meets the heart line, the person loves dallience.
51. If there is cross on this line below the mount of Mercury, the person has to face failure in business again and again.
52. If several squares are formed by this line, the person is quite a genius but he remains unsuccessful in his work.
53. If the heart line gets divided in several branches under the mount of Jupiter, the person is very lucky.
54. If there is a cluster of branches from the very start of this line, the person is very talkative.
55. If this line has a cluster of branches in the middle, the person is obstinate and proud.
56. If a person has no heart line on his hand, he will be cruel.
57. If no subsidiary lines branch off from the heart line, the person has no child.
58. If this line is under the mount of Jupiter, without any lines branching off, the person remains poor in life.

59. If there is some other sign at the finishing end, the person becomes a victim of paralysis.
60. If there is a point under the mount of Sun, the person is very emotional.
61. If any sign is seen under the mount of Mercury, the person will be a famous physician.
62. If the sign of circle is felt on the line, then the person's heart is weak.
63. If any island is seen on the heart line, the person gets cheated several times in life.
64. If an island is visible on both heart and head lines, the person will be lascivious and immoral.
65. If there is some sign of injury on the heart line, the person will have to face failure in love.
66. The more distinct, beautiful and reddish the heart line is, the greater the successes and excellence, the person will get in his life.
67. If the finishing end of the heart line is divided into two parts, then such a person will be a successful judge. He will be generous, virtuous and social.

In fact, the heart line has a very great importance in a person's life and it is necessary for the palmists to study this line carefully.

The Sun Line

This line is called the *Sun Line* in English and in Hindi, it is called *Yash Line*. Everyone has a desire to do something in his life which may be appreciated in the society. People may respect his or her ideas and his or her fame may remain imperishable even after his death. It is very necessary to take the help of the Sun line for studying all this. This Sun line is instrumental in providing honour, respect, prosperity and popularity to a person. If the health, heart and life lines are sufficiently strong in one's hand, still if the Sun line is weak, the person's life remains almost negligible. Only distinct, deep and faultless Sun line helps a person to rise high. It is necessary for a palmist to study this line minutely.

In the opinion of learned palmists, only the the Sun line on the hand is not be given the sole importance because the Sun line is not able to exert its influence till the fate line is strong on a palm. Therefore, fate line should also be studied while studying the Sun line.

I have experienced that all persons do not have the Sun line in their palms and it is also correct that the place of origin of the Sun line is different in different hands. Its influence is denoted by its length and clarity. So, while observing the hand, the place of the Sun line should also be noted particularly.

This Sun line is under the mount of Sun. This can be easily recognised as it always terminates at the mount of Sun, whatever be its origin. The line which does not reach the mount of Sun, cannot be called the Sun line. I am making the place of origin of this line clear for the benefit of my readers:

1. In some hands, this line starts from the mount of Venus and reaches the mount of Sun.
2. On some palms, this line starts from the end of the life line and goes up to the mount of Sun.

3. Its place of origin is sometimes the mount of Mars. It starts from here and reaches the mount of Sun after cutting the heart line.
4. On some hands, this line starts from the head line and touches the mount of Sun.
5. Its place of origin has been seen from the heart line also. From here, it goes up to the mount of Sun.
6. Sometimes this starts from the area of Harshala and reaches the mount of Sun.
7. Sometimes this line starts from the mount of Moon and is seen proceeding towards the mount of Sun.
8. On some hands, this line starts from the wrist, reaches the mount of Sun after cutting all the lines on its path.
9. It has been found reaching the root of the finger of Apollo starting from the mount of Dragon's Tail.
10. Several times, its place of origin has been found to be the area of Dragon's Head.
11. On some palms, this line starts from the centre of the palm and reaches the mount of Sun.
12. On some hands, this line succeeds in reaching the mount of Sun after starting from the mount of Mercury.

As far as I know, this line has these places of origin but this line can have other sources also. The readers, however should bear in mind that only *that line can be recognised as Sun line which terminates on the mount of Sun.*

I am now describing in brief the Sun line which originates from different places:

First Position

This line starts from the mount of Venus and reaches the mount of Sun. Such a line is considered very favourable in itself. A person with such a line is financially very prosperous. He has affairs with several other women besides his wife in his life and gains wealth from them or such a person gets much money from the parents of his wife. In truth, these persons become lucky only after marriage. Correctly speaking, their fate rises due to their beloved ones or their mistresses. Several times such persons get adopted which brings them much wealth.

Second Position

Such a line is visible in very few hands but those who have such a line are high class artists and are greatly emotional. At the same time, they amass much wealth through arts. Their luck is bright in itself. By nature, such persons are sentimental, social and attractive.

Third Position

Such persons reach a high position in police or in army if this line is seen on their palms and get State or National awards for their meritorious services. Though such persons succeed with their own efforts, yet they achieve their aim by persevering gradually.

Fourth Position

Such persons are prominent intellectuals. They are high class scientists, philosophers and logicians. They get complete success in any task they undertake in their lives and use their sharp intellect in every field. Their works are important in themselves. Their fortune rises at the age of 28 and they get special respect and fame in the society.

Fifth Position

Persons having this kind of line on their palms attain complete success in life. Though it is true that their earlier life is quite full of troubles but they rise so much with their own efforts that people get wonder-struck. At the age of 45, their fame and respect reach at a very high level. Their work is done in a miraculous manner and they get everlasting praise even after their death. But if this line gets broken in its path, the person has to face blame in life.

Sixth Position

Such a person has to work very hard in life. Neither does he get education in a proper way nor does he get any help to enable him to rise in life. Whatever success such persons get, it is all due to their own efforts. Still such persons in later stage become judges, barristers and eminent educationists. They undertake foreign travels many times in their life, at the same time get defamed in foreign countries due to love affairs.

Seventh Position

The luck of such persons shines after their marriage. They rise in a wonderful manner after marriage. They succeed in their work and are able to collect capability to reach their goals. Such persons are emotional, kind-hearted and lovers. They love pomp and show and luxurious living. They create and maintain false environment around them.

Eighth Position

Such a Sun line is found in the hands of very few persons. There is no dearth of money, respect, position, fame, prosperity, popularity, etc. in their lives. Such persons lead a simple life and have deep faith in religion. Such persons are high class tradesmen and successful writers.

Ninth Position

A person having beautiful, distinct and reddish line on his palm, passes a very happy childhood. There is no dearth of money and luxury in his life. Such persons do not have to work hard in life. They go on getting success in life with a little effort. Such persons are high class traders. There is one defect in such persons that they keep contacts with low class persons which results in diminishing their respect in the society. But these persons do not care for the society nor do they have any kind of check on themselves.

Tenth Position

Persons on whose hands this kind of Sun line is found are clever and zealous. They reach the very bottom of the matter immediately and can read the thoughts of the person sitting in front by looking at his face only. They remain independent-minded in life. Once they take a decision, they stick to it and act fully according to it. Such persons are called successful individuals and excellent friends.

Eleventh Position

Those who have such a Sun line are strongly fortunate. They get sudden wealth many times in their lives. They do not lack anything in their materialistic life. They can be called happy and prosperous from all angles.

Twelfth Position

This kind of Sun line is found in the hands of very few persons. Persons having this line in their hands are successful actors and earn matchless money and fame by means of their art.

Now, I am placing some new facts before the readers in connection with the Sun line:

1. Long, distinct and straight Sun line helps a person to get fame, respect and honour.
2. If this line is clearly seen on both the hands, the person will get complete success in life.
3. If this line is complete in its length without any cuts, the person will not be found wanting for anything in his life.
4. A small Sun line is helpful for success in life after hard work and struggles.
5. If the palm is deep and the Sun line is distinct, the capability of the person is not correctly utilized.
6. The person changes his work or trade at an age where the Sun line gets cut.
7. If this line is thin and faint, the person is not able to fully utilize his art.
8. The person gets bankrupt in life and gets defamed in society if there is a sign of island in the path of the Sun line.
9. If the mount of Jupiter is prominent on the palm and the Sun line is deep, the person has contacts with people of very high class.
10. If there is a star sign on the Sun line, the person can attain worldwide success by means of his art.
11. A person gets particular wealth at an age where the Sun line is deepest on the palm.

12. If there is a sign of a point at the termination of the Sun line, the person has to face many troubles in life and gets success at the end.
13. If the Sun line is thin but is straight and distinct, the person becomes prosperous.
14. If the sign of a star is seen at the end of the Sun line, the person gets worldwide honour.
15. If the sign of a star is found at the beginning and at the end of the Sun line, the person does not lack anything in his life.
16. If the Sun line ends with several smaller lines, the person gets failures in his life.
17. If the Sun line terminates in the form of a curved line, the person is not able to make progress in life.
18. If there is a cross sign at the end of the Sun line, the person's end is extremely painful.
19. If the Sun line is broken at several places, then though there is genius in the person yet he is not able to earn good amount of money and does not get high class respect.
20. If the Sun line is absent, the person's life remains useless.
21. If the sign of square is seen on the Sun line, the person gets insulted several times in his life.
22. If this line starts from the life line on both the hands, the person can get success by means of arts.
23. If the Sun line ends in two branches or it gets divided into two lines towards the end, the person is not respected in the society.
24. If several other subsidiary lines are seen along with the Sun line, the person rises extraordinarily in life.
25. If the Sun line is cut by the marriage line, then his married life remains completely unhappy.
26. If any line proceeds from the Sun line towards the head line, the person will get plenty of wealth in life.
27. If there is sign of rectangle on this line, the person will get many failures in the beginning but will get complete success in the end.

28. If three or four lines cut this line, the person cannot be successful in anything in life.
29. If any line starts from the mount of Saturn and cuts the Sun line, the person cannot succeed in life due to paucity of wealth.
30. If this line is distinct but some zig-zag lines are seen with it, the person's attributes are taken advantage of.
31. If the Sun line is deep and on both sides if there are subsidiary lines, the person gets high honour.
32. If any line goes towards the mount of Saturn after starting from the Sun line, the person is able to get special qualities of this mount.
33. If any line starts from the Sun line and reaches the mount of Jupiter, the person gets high government position.
34. If several small lines are seen near this line, the person experiences hindrance in his economic life.
35. If any line starts from the heart line, forms into a trident and touches the Sun line, the person succeeds with his own efforts in his life.
36. If the finger of Apollo is curved but the Sun line is clear, the person gets credit for committing offences.
37. If three lines are visible towards the end of the Sun line, the person does not suffer from paucity of wealth.
38. If this line proceeds mostly in a broken state, the person is not able to attain success due to his laziness.
39. If this line is chained, the person has to face many difficulties in his life.
40. If this line is zig-zag, the person's own acts create hindrances in his life.
41. If both the head line and the Sun line are excellent on the palm, the person's life is excellent in every way.
42. If there is an island at the end of the line, the person remains sick all his life.

In fact, the Sun line proves very useful in studying the life and fate of a person. So a palmist should study the Sun line very minutely and with depth.

◆◆

The Fate Line

Though everything goes on in life but a person's whole life gets spoiled in a way if the fate does not support him. A person's life becomes inactive and useless in a way if luck does not favour him though he may possess a grand personality, be very charitable at heart and enjoys an excellent health. It is said that if luck favours a person, then even the soil turns into gold by his very touch. On the contrary, if the luck does not favour him, then even gold turns into soil by his touch.

In fact, the importance of luck is considered highest in life, so the fate line is considered significant in the palm. The excellence of fate is related to the depth, distinctiveness and faultlessness of the fate line. If all the lines on a person's hand are defective and weak but his fate line is excellent in itself, then it is certain that all his vices are hidden and he succeeds in making progress in his life. Therefore, it is necessary for a palmist to study carefully the fate line while studying the palm.

This fate line is not found in all hands and my experience is that this fate line is absent nearly on fifty percent hands. But by saying this, I do not mean that a person is unlucky as he does not have fate line nor can he succeed by making efforts and is unfortunate if the fate line is absent. A person can turn things in his favour with a little effort and genius.

This line can be called the Saturn line also as this line terminates at the mount of Saturn. Though this line starts from different places on different hands, it invariably ends at the mount of Saturn. This is why it is also known as Saturn line.

If this line is weak on a person's hands or is absent, such a person though he rises in life, yet he does not get any cooperation from his brothers, relatives, etc. Whatever progress he makes, he does it by his own efforts. Such persons do not get any cooperation from the society nor any help from the family. If the Saturn line is absent on a person's hands, then it should be understood that all that is visible in his life has been possible only due to his own efforts.

This line proceeds from below and goes upwards and as I have explained earlier, this line has different places of its origin but this line invariably terminates at the mount of Saturn. A person's desires, feelings, his mental and intellectual standard and an estimation of his capabilities can be made known by means of this line. It can be known with the help of fate line how high will the person rise in his life. What will be his financial position in life? Will he be able to get wealth, respect, position, honour, etc. in his life? Is his life full of worries? Can the person overcome those difficulties and attain success? All these facts can be known by means of the fate line alone.

The mount of Saturn is situated at the root of the finger of Saturn. Any line which starts from any part of the palm and touches the mount of Saturn is called the fate line. It exerts different influences of its origin from different places on the palm. So, both the source and termination points of the fate line should be studied carefully and minutely.

If this line orginates from anywhere and reaches the mount of Saturn without support then such a line is considered undoubtedly strong and excellent. But in case, the fate line crosses the mount of Saturn and tries to reach the phalange of the finger of Saturn, then such a line is considered faulty.

I have elucidated some facts about the fate line. According to my experience, the sources of fate line can be as follows:
1. The fate line starts from above the wrist and taking help of other lines on the palm, reaches the mount of Saturn.
2. Several times this line starts from near the life line and reaches the mount of Saturn.
3. The fate line starts from the mount of Venus and reaches the mount of Saturn.
4. Sometimes this line appears to start from the mount of Mars also.
5. This line tries to reach the mount of Saturn after crossing the life line.
6. 1 have seen this line starting from the area of Dragon's Head on some hands.

7. I have observed the fate line starting from the heart line and reaching the mount of Saturn.
8. Several times, this line proceeds upto the area of Neptune and the mount of Saturn.
9. In some hands, this line starts from the mount of Moon also.
10. The source of this line has also been seen from the area of Harshala.
11. Several times, this line has been seen originating from the head line and proceeding towards the mount of Saturn.

I have shown 11 places of origin of the fate line above. In most hands, the source of this line is as given above but there can be other sources as well.

In the following pages, I am describing the forecasts pertaining to different places of origin of the fate line.

The First Position

This kind of fate line is considered the best. It is called excellent and gets importance if it is distinct, deep and faultless. It should always be kept in mind that the fate line is considered auspicious if it reaches the mount of Saturn, but if it crosses the mount of Saturn, then it gives opposite results. On some hands, I have seen this line reaching the second phalange of the finger of Saturn. But this kind of line indicates that the person will have too many ambitions and desires, he will not be able to see the fulfilment of his desires in his life. This over-long line spoils the completed works of the person.

It is said to be giving auspicious results if this line does not climb over the finger of Saturn but stops at the fate line, divides into two as it proceeds towards the mount of Staturn. Then it is an indication of special success. A person reaches a very high position in his life if the fate line at its end divides into two parts, one part of Saturn while the other end reaches the mount of Jupiter. Such persons have been found to reach high position though born in ordinary families.

A person has to meet hindrances in his life if slanting lines cut the fate line at the mount of Saturn. He is able to succeed inspite of many obstacles. The lesser these lines of obstructions are, the better it is considered.

If the source of fate line is below the wrist, then such a line is also considered faulty. Such person leads an unfortunate and poor life.

The Second Position

According to the science of Palmistry, this kind of line is also considered excellent but if this kind of line tries to climb over the finger of Saturn, then this creates difficulties. Such persons are surrounded with worries even though they are courageous. Such persons get success in life with great difficulty.

If this kind of line reaches the mount of Saturn, the person rises with his own efforts, though he has to face many difficulties in his childhood. His fate rises fully in the 28th year of his age.

Such persons are of reserve nature and do not succeed in taking quick decisions. If this kind of fate line has slanting lines on it then the person has to face many hindrances several times in his life and is able to succeed only after best efforts.

If the life line is also proceeding along with the fate line then it is not considered auspicious. The combination or intermingling of fate line and life line is not considered favourable.

The Third Position

This line is considered as auspicious as it is distinct. If this line proceeds after cutting the life line then the person has to face many difficulties at the time where this line cuts the life line. In this condition the person can get injured in dangerous accident, become insolvent or commit suicide.

This line starts from the mount of Venus. It is, therefore, clear that fortune of that person will begin to shine after his marriage. Such a person is highly advanced in matters of love and gets much money from the parents of his wife. The wife of such a person is beautiful, attractive and leads a life of pomp. But the old age of such a person is full of troubles. His married life is not considered happy. If an island is seen in the middle of the fate line, then the husband and the wife are not able to adjust and live together due to differences of opinion.

The Fourth Position

This fate line is also considered auspicious but the rise of fortune is possible only after youth. He has to meet hindrances in the field of education and is not able to get higher education.

If there is no subsidiary line along with this type of fate line, the person goes on repenting on his own mistakes. He is not able to get the cooperation of friends. He has to work very hard to rise high in life. Luck smiles on him rather late and he is able to rise only with the help of others. Such a person can rise high in police or in the army.

The Fifth Position

This position of the fate line on the palm is said to be favourable but if it tries to reach the end of the finger of Saturn, the person cannot achieve success in life. Though he constantly tries to go ahead, yet he faces failure again and again in life. He can rise only with the help of an important person.

Such persons make progress in the middle of their age. They are successful painters or writers. What I mean to suggest is that they are experts in a particular area.

If such a line gets broken or becomes zig-zag after proceeding beyond the life line, the person is not able to rise and goes on cursing his fate constantly. If such a line is cut by vertical or horizontal lines, then he has to face difficulties in his life. Such persons are successful patriots and their old age is very comfortable.

The Sixth Position

A person having this kind of line on his hand is considered very lucky. The rise of fortune of such a person starts after the age of 36. He makes wonderful progress between the age of 36 and 42.

The early part of life of such a person is very painful. His youth and his old age are considered very comfortable and in later years of his life, he gets wealth, fame, honour and respect.

If such a line is broken at places on its path, then the person has to meet with difficulties and if there is sign of a square on the line, then he is called unlucky. A person can become completely successful in life if any subsidiary line branches off from the fate line and proceeds towards the mount of Jupiter.

The Seventh Position

This fate line starts from the heart line and directly reaches the mount of Saturn but in some persons, this line takes the form of a trident, one end of which goes to the mount of Sun while the other towards the mount of Jupiter. Such a fate line is considered very auspicious. If this line divides itself into two parts near its end, the person will get plenty of wealth, respect, fame, position and honour in his life time.

Such a person is sympathetic and always helps others in his life. He earns crores of rupees by his own efforts and spends them in religious matters. If there is a sign of an island in the beginning of this line he has to face much blames in his life. If this line gets broken in its path, the person has to bear much financial loss at that part of his age. If there are zig-zag lines on this line the person has to struggle several times in his life and he is able to obtain success after facing great difficulties.

The Eighth Position

If this line is faultless, distinct and deep, the person passes his childhood very comfortably. From the study point of view, he gets the best education. Such boys have sharp intellect and they are singled out for their independent ideas. Though they don't get any special cooperation from their family, yet they try and go ahead towards attaining success. Such persons are successful judges, writers or philosophers. The family life of such persons can be completely happy.

They are fated to go to foreign countries several times in their life but if this kind of fate line is broken or zig-zag, the person has a very few chances of success in life. He has to struggle in life again and again and is able to succeed after a lot of efforts. If such a line divides itself into two at the end then this is an auspicious indication and such a person surely succeeds in achieving his aims.

The Ninth Position

Such fate line is considered very auspicious. If this line gets divided into two or three parts on reaching the mount of Saturn, the person becomes owner of inestimable wealth and rises very high in life. Such a person has more than one sources of income in his life. If the extreme end of such a line proceeds towards the mount of Jupiter, the person can attain high position and get good results by means of literature. If this kind of end is proceeding towards the mount of Sun, the person can attain full succcess by trading with foreign countries. He takes keen interest in religious matters and gets respectable position in the society.

If this kind of line is broken or chain-like, then the person has to face many difficulties in his life. If this line seems to ride over the phalange of the finger of Saturn, the person will have to bear too much loss.

Persons with this kind of line on their hands become lucky after marriage. They are of unsteady nature and are fickle-minded. They have affairs with more than one woman in their life. They are fated for several voyages in life. Such persons are of loving nature, sweet-tongued and like to remain aloof.

The Tenth Position

Persons having this kind of fate line on their hands certainly reach a high position. Such a person undertakes foreign travel several times in his life or he becomes a high ranking authority in air force. Such a person gets national honour in life. He is not at all wanting in courage or patience in life. If such a line is chained, zig-zag or broken, the person has to face too many difficulties in life. If such a fate line gets divided into two parts, one end of which goes towards the mount of Sun, the other end goes towards the mount of Jupiter, then the person is extremely fortunate.

The Eleventh Position

Such fate line is very rarely found. The individuality of such a person is excellent in itself. They shine in life like the Venus. The society is influenced by their work. They wield significant influence in directing the country. Their thoughts and actions are all well-planned.

Having born in an ordinary family, such a person is efficient, able and happy from all points of view.

If such a line gets divided into two parts towards the end then he is a high official and there is no dearth of anything in his life from the materialistic point of view.

I have explained eleven kinds of sources of the fate line but there can be other places of origin also. Readers should keep one thing in mind that *any line which touches the mount of Saturn is the only line worth being called the Fate Line in reality.*

If there are more than one fate line on one's hands and both lines end on the mount of Saturn, then the combined effect of both these lines can be seen in the life of the person. If small lines branch off towards the end of the Saturn line and the fate line, then these lines indicate the high ambitions of the person. If such lines are seen leaning downwards, then the person has to face many difficulties in life.

In the following pages, I am explaining some new facts connected with the fate line :

1. If the fate line is straight and distinct and is proceeding towards the mount of Sun after passing over the mount of Saturn, the person will get special success in arts.
2. If this line is red in colour and reaches the first phalange of the finger of Saturn, the person will die of accident.
3. If this line becomes like a chain while cutting the heart line, the person will get defamed in love matters.
4. If the fate line (in the centre of the palm) is faint or thin and indistinct, the youth of the person will be full of troubles.
5. If there are subsidiary lines along with the fate line on a person's hands, then he will be highly respected.
6. If the fate line is chain- like or zig-zag, the person has to bear great troubles in life.
7. If a person has no fate line on his hands, his life is very ordinary and negligible.
8. If the fate line is zig-zag from the very beginning, the childhood of the person is very troublesome.
9. If the fate line starts from its source and bends towards a particular mount or any subsidiary line branches off from

the mount of Saturn and proceeds towards a particular mount, then the person gets the benefit of this mount also in his life.

10. If the fate line abruptly comes to an end, the person has to suffer many difficulties in his life.
11. A person gets special benefit or advantage at the time of life where this line is deep, faultless and distinct.
12. A person has to face difficulties and his life takes a turn as many times as the fate line breaks on the palm.
13. If the fate line starts from the wrist and climbs over the finger of Saturn, the person is unfortunate. If the fate line is like this, he will not get any comfort or happiness in his life.
14. If the fate line is below the first bracelet, i.e., its origin is below the first bracelet, then the person has to bear too many troubles in his life.
15. If there is any other subsidiary line along with the fate line, then it is called auspicious. If the fingers are long and the source of the fate line is at the mount of Moon, then the person is a famous exorcist.
16. If the fate line proceeds after cutting the mount of Moon, then the person undertakes journeys to foreign countries several times.
17. If there is a sign of triangle at the source of the fate line, the person rises with his own intellect.
18. If some lines branch off from the fate line and go upwards, the person gains inestimable wealth.
19. If the fate line commences from the head line and there are zig-zag lines on its path, the person gets success in his old age.
20. If the fate line turns into a square on the mount of Saturn, the person gets success in life after hard work.
21. If the fate line commences from the head line and its branches go upto the mount of Mercury, Jupiter and Sun, the person is famous internationally.
22. If three or four lines are branching off from the source of the fate line, the person's fate rises in foreign countries.

23. If a subsidiary line goes towards the mount of Venus from the source of the fate line, then the person's fate smiles upon him through some women.
24. If the fate line terminates near the head line, the person has to face frustration again and again in his life.
25. The horizontal and vertical lines on fate line are all a hindrance in its advancement.
26. If there is a sign of star at the end of the fate line, his old age is extremely troublesome.
27. If the fate line and marriage line both get combined, the person's family life is unhappy.
28. If any subsidiary line branches off from the fate line, then it helps to make the fate stronger.
29. If there are branches above and under this line, then he will have to bear financial troubles.
30. If there is a cross or net at the end of this line, he will be murdered mercilessly.
31. If there is a rectangle at the end of the line, the person will have special faith in religion.
32. The sign of plus on fate line is considered auspicious.
33. If the fate line is deep, distinct and reddish, then the person makes quick progress in life.

In fact, the gist of life is in one's fate. So, one who has strong, clear and beautiful fate line, progresses quickly because of his fate and gets an honourable place in the society and enjoys fully all the material happiness of life.

◆◆

The Health Line

The importance of health is considered supreme in a man's life. A man may possess fame, respect, high post, honour and luxuries but if he is not healthy then all his prosperity is useless in a way. Therefore, the ancient scriptures have accepted *health as the best of wealths*. A palmist should, first of all, study the health line after studying the life line.

Good health affects the whole life of a person and all his works. If the health is good, he can do all the works. He can put in all the mental and physical power in his every work. But, if the health does not help him, then his life becomes useless in a way.

The source of health line can be at any place on the palm but it is certain that it must terminate at the mount of Mercury. Several times it has been observed that a line starts and tries to proceed towards the mount of Mercury but it cannot reach it. It can only be called the health line if it touches or reaches the mount of Mercury. Some lines just touch the mount of Mercury. So, such lines also can be accepted as Mercury line or Health line.

This line can commence from any part of the palm. Chiefly, it starts from the following places:

1. From the mount of Venus.
2. Near the life line.
3. Near the heart line.
4. From the mount of Moon or Luna.
5. From the Bracelets.
6. From the Fate line.
7. From the mount of Mars.

I have stated above the places from where the health line can commence on the palm but it must terminate on the mount of Mercury.

This line should be carefully studied. The concerned person's health is as good and of high order as the line on the palm is distinct, faultless and deep. His body is well-formed and pesonality effective. If the health line on the palm is broken or cut, dispersed, zig-zag or chain-like, then the person's health will be weak in itself. He will not be able to enjoy anything in his life. It is extremely necessary for the health line to be distinct on the palm.

On some palms, the absence of the health line is also seen. My experience in this connection is that the absence of the health line in itself is a good indication. Persons not having health lines on their hands are healthy, attractive and lead a happy and comfortable life. Such persons remain immune from any kind of disease and prepared to do anything on the strength of their courage.

A person's health remains life-long weak if this line is wide on the palm. If this line is joined as the links of a chain the, person suffers from stomach troubles throughout his life. If this line moves up like a wave, the person will surely suffer from liver disorder. The yellowishness of this line indicates that the person will remain afflicted with jaundice or some other disease connected with blood. A person's health remains as bad as the number of spots are found on the health line. If the health line is found cut at several places on the palm the person remains sick all his life.

In the following pages some other facts about health line are being explained :

1. If the health line is not mixed with the life line, the person has longevity.
2. A person's health is said to be excellent if the health line is long, faultless and strong.
3. If the health line begins with a reddish tinge, the person suffers from heart disease in his life.
4. If this line is red in the middle, the person's health remains weak throughout his life.
5. If this line is red towards the end, the peson has to suffer constantly from headache.
6. If this line is of many colours, the person has to face paralysis in his life.

7. If the line is of yellow colour, the person has diseases of secret organs.
8. If the health line passes the mount of Moon and proceeds on the side of the palm and reaches the mount of Mercury, the person goes to foreign countries several times in his life.
9. If this line is thin and distinct and the head line is strong, the person's memory is very sharp.
10. If there are spots on this line and on the head line, the person remains sick throughout his life.
11. If the health line is of red colour on the palm, the person is too much lascivious and indulgent.
12. If the head line is weak and the health line is wavy, the person suffers constantly from stomach diseases.
13. If this line gets cut on reaching the mount of Mercury, the person has defective bile.
14. If this line is of red colour and moves forward to the heart line, the person's heart may be considered very weak.
15. If the health line makes a cross on the heart line, the person suffers from dyspepsia.
16. If several subsidiary lines branch off and go upwards then the person's health is considered very excellent.
17. If the health line is long and waving but the fate line is weak, the person suffers from diseases of the teeth.
18. If the health line is weak and the heart line too is weak, the person is weak-willed.
19. If there is sign of a rectangle at the end of the health line, the person suffers from asthma.
20. If the fingers are angled and the health line is weak, the person suffers from paralysis.
21. If several small lines are seen going downwards from the health line, the person's health remains weak throughout his life.
22. If any branch line is going towards the mount of Sun from the health line, the person has uncountable wealth.
23. If any subsidiary of the health line goes towards the mount of Saturn, the person is sober, reflective and long-lived.

24. If the Moon line comes and meets the health line, the person is a successful poet and travels to foreign countries several times.
25. If any subsidiary line after making a semicircle proceeds towards the mount of Mars, the person is a successful foreteller.
26. If the health line cuts the heart line on the palm of a man, the person suffers from epilepsy.
27. If wavy health line touches the fate line, the person's luck remains weak throughout his life.
28. If such a line touches the head line, the person's mind is very weak.
29. If wavy health line touches the mount of Sun, the person gets defamed several times in his life.
30. If the health line is wavy and crosses the mount of Mercury, the person has to bear a very heavy loss in business.
31. If the fingers are pointed and there is absence of health line on the palm, the person will be active.
32. If the mount of Mercury is quite broken and the health line is absent, the person is of happy disposition.
33. If wavy Mercury line turns and proceeds towards the mount of Venus, the person gets a great shock in love affairs.
34. If the sign of an island is seen on the health line, the person suffers from diseases connected with blood and his lungs are weak.
35. If there are several small lines near the health line, the person's health always remains weak.
36. If the health line goes beyond the life line and touches the head line and the heart line and proceeds further, the person remains weak in his life.
37. If this line is joined to the life line and there are blue spots on the line, the person complains of heart trouble.
38. If there is a cross at the end of the head line and the health line, the person is very much successful.
39. If the health line is bright at some places and faint at other places or is divided into pieces, then his health remains weak all through his life.

40. If the health line is weak and is very thin, then laziness is seen on his face all the time.
41. If the health line and the Sun line have established in relationship, the person's brain is very fertile.
42. If there is a cross at the end of this line and the sign of cross is also there on the head line, the person becomes blind in his life.
43. If an oblique line cuts the health line anywhere on its path, there is very severe accident on that part of the age.
44. If there is a sign of star on the line, he does not get cooperation of the family during his life.
45. If there is sign of cross near the health line, accidents take place several times in his life.
46. If there is an island sign on the health line, while passing over the region of Dragon's Head, the person suffers from tuberculosis.
47. If there is sign of island on the head line and the health line passes over this island, the person's health will be very weak in life.
48. If the fate line is cut and there is a sign of island on the health line, the person remains worried financially.
49. A person has diseases of secret organs if the health line is situated deep in the palm.
50. A cross on the health line indicates unsound health.
51. If there are stars on the health line, the person cannot enjoy family happiness.
52. If both the line of Mercury and the love line are intermingled with one another, the person's wife's health remains weak all through her life.
53. If the health line is distinct on both hands, the person is indulgent and lascivious.
54. If the health line is dual, the person is a master of good luck.
55. If double health line touches the mount of Sun also, then the person gets very high post in politics.
56. If the health line and heart line meet together under the mount of Mercury, then the person dies of heart attack.

57. If any subsidiary line also proceeds along with the health line, the person's health should be considered very excellent.
58. If the health line is good but there are yellow lines on the nails, the person will die untimely.
59. If the health line is strong from underneath and gets fainter from above as it proceeds, the person dies in his youth.
60. If the health line commences from the bracelet but is broken then the person is to die soon.
61. If there is sign of a net on the health line then the person does not enjoy full age.
62. If the health line and the life line get combined and there is sign of star above it, the person dies while on travel.
63. If the nails are too long, the person suffers from neurosis.
64. If the colour of nails is blue, the person suffers from paralysis. If nails are small and the health line is cut, the person suffers from epilepsy.
65. If the health line is weak and the Mercury line is wavy, the person suffers from rheumatism.
66. Good health line is said to be comfortable from all points of view for an individual.

A palmist should carefully study the health line. With the help of this line, future sickness and accidents can be known beforehand and he can make a person careful by giving such warnings.

In fact, the health line is of much importance on the palm. There cannot be two opinions about this.

The Marriage Line

The softest and a wonderful organ in our body is called the 'heart'. In a way it has the greatest importance in the body. On one side it supplies blood to the whole body while on the other, it is so delicate that it keeps carefully in itself all the emotions of life. Delicate ideas, feelings towards the opposite sex, etc. are conveyed by means of this organ. It is so delicate that it breaks or gets hurt by a very small adverse happening. It is a beautiful embodiment of human imagination. Compassion, kindness, affection and love feelings, etc. are propagated by means of this organ.

Our heart desires to establish contacts with the other heart and both desire to love each other. Both the hearts are brimming with sweet feelings and when both of them are bound together in a string, the society calls it the 'institution of marriage'.

A person's life is said to be complete only when his or her other half is beautiful, wise, full of love feelings and both hearts are capable to completely unite with one another. If a man has a gentle, beautiful, healthy and educated wife, then such a house is considered more comfortable than even the palace of God Indra. Therefore, a palmist should give equal importance to the life line and to the marriage line because the study of only this line enables a complete study of a man's life.

The life journey of a person is full of thorns. To cross this path, such a companion is needed who helps when in trouble, gives courage when faced with troubles and is able to proceed with heart and soul together in life.

Though the marriage line or line of love appears very small, yet it has the greatest significance. The horizontal lines under the little finger, above the heart line, alongside the mount of Mercury, which are seen coming out of the palm, are called the marriage lines.

There can be three or four such lines on the palm but one line is chief among all these. These are called the marriage lines. If they are above the heart line then such a person surely gets married. In case these lines are under the heart line the person does not get married in life.

The line which is longest, healthy and strong, should be taken as the marriage line if there are 2 or 3 lines on the palm. Other lines are indicative of the fact that either previously made engagements will get broken or there will be affairs with other women after marriage.

But there are other small lines along with this and these are called 'love lines'. The men will have as many affairs with women as is the number of such lines. This also applies in the case of women.

But one should not make up his mind only by seeing these lines; study of mounts along with it is also necessary. If there are such lines and the mount of Jupiter is very prominent, the person can surely establish love contacts but his love is platonic and blameless. If the mount of Saturn is very prominent and there are such lines, the person establishes love contacts with women elder in age to him. If the mount of Sun is prominent on the palm and there are such lines, the person establishes love contacts with women after careful thoughts. If the mount of Mercury is prominent and the love lines are visible on the palm, the person will get money from his mistresses. If there are love lines on the palm and the mount of Moon is prominent, the person will be indulgent, lascivious and will run after beautiful women. If the mount of Venus is very prominent and there are love lines, the person establishes sex contacts with several women in his life and gains full success in it.

Love line has intimate connection with the heart line. He will establish love contact at as early an age as is the nearness of love lines to the heart line. The farther the distance between love lines and the heart line, the more late will he establish the relationship with the other sex.

If there is no love line on the palm, the person remains constrained and does not become indulgent.

If the love line is deep and distinct, the person's love contacts also will be deep. But if the love lines are small and weak, the person's love contacts will also be of short duration.

It should be understood that he will have affairs with two women simultaneously if two love lines are proceeding side by side. If there is a sign of cross on the love line, then his love affair also breaks. If there is sign of an island on the love lines, then he bears defamation in his love affairs. If the love line is proceeding onward to the mount of Sun, the person will have love affairs in high families. If the love line gets divided into two parts, the person's love affairs end abruptly. If any subsidiary line from the love lines is proceeding downwards, the person will face blame in love affairs. If any subsidiary line from the love line moves upwards, the person's love affair remains ever lasting and he enjoys it life-long. If the love line is broken on its way, the love matters also get broken in between.

Now, I am explaining some facts in connection with the marriage line for my readers:

1. If the marriage line is distinct, faultless and reddish, the person's married life will be happy and comfortable.
2. If the marriage line is strong in both the hands, the person gets full success in his married life.
3. If the marriage line reaches the second phalange of the little finger, the person remains unmarried throughout his life.
4. If the marriage line bends downwards and touches the heart line, the person's wife will die before him.
5. If the marriage line appears to be broken, then either the wife will die or will get divorced in the middle of the person's life.
6. If any line moves forward from the mount of Venus and establishes contact with the marriage line, then his married life will be very troublesome.
7. If the marriage line proceeds ahead and becomes two pronged, then the person's married life cannot be called happy; on the other hand his married life becomes full of conflicts.
8. If any line branches off from the marriage line and proceeds towards the heart line, then his wife remains with him all his life.
9. If the marriage line is wide, the person will have no zeal about the marriage.

10. If the marriage line divides into two parts as it proceeds onwards and one of its branches touches the heart line, the person will establish marriage contacts with his sister-in-law in addition to his wife.
11. If the marriage line gets divided into several parts as it proceeds onwards, the person's married life is very troublesome.
12. If the marriage line touches the head line, then the person will kill his wife. If the marriage line gets divided into several parts on the mount of Mercury, then the engagements get broken several times.
13. If the marriage line moves downwards after coming into contact with the Sun line, then such a marriage is said to be unequal.
14. If one branch of the marriage line reaches the mount of Venus after leaning downwards, the person's wife is corrupt.
15. If there is a black spot on the marriage line, then the person cannot have good terms with his wife.
16. If any marriage line cuts the life line on proceeding onwards, the person's married life will be artistic.
17. If the marriage line, the fate line and the head line meet together, the person's married life will be very troublesome.
18. If any oblique line cuts the marriage line, the person's married life will be full of difficulties.
19. If any other line joins the marriage line, the person's married life gets spoiled due to his beloved.
20. If there is a sign of island visible in the beginning of the marriage line, the person gets married after many difficulties.
21. If there is a cross sign at the place where the marriage line leans, the person's wife dies unexpectedly.
22. If the children's line cuts the marriage line, the person's marriage takes place after great difficulties.
23. If there are more than one islands on the marriage line, the person will remain a bachelor all his life.
24. If there are two or three other lines moving along with the marriage line near the region of Mercury, the person has

sexual relationships with 2 or 3 other women in addition to his wife.
25. If the marriage line moves onwards and bends towards the little finger, the life partner dies prior to him.
26. Abrupt break of marriage line should be taken to be full of difficulties in family life.
27. If there are two parallel lines on the region of Mercury then the person will have two marriages.
28. If the marriage lines meet the Sun line after moving onwards, his wife will be highly posted in service.
29. If there are two heart lines, the person will get married after great difficulties.
30. If a line coming from the mount of Moon meets the line of marriage, then the person is indulgent, lascivious and has secret love affairs.
31. If any line comes from the line of Mars and meets the marriage line, then there are constant hindrances in his marriage.
32. The vertical lines on the marriage line are called children's lines or lines of progeny.
33. The children's lines are very fine and it is not possible to see these with naked eyes.
34. The long and prominent lines among these children's lines indicate sons but the weak and thin lines can be attributed to daughters.
35. If any of the lines is broken, then it indicates the child's death.
36. If the bracelet is weak and the mount of Venus is not developed, then such a person cannot get the happiness of children.
37. If the lines are straight and distinct, the children are healthy but if the lines are weak, then the children will also be weak.
38. Taking the marriage line denoting 60 years, the part where it is deep at that age, the person gets married.

In fact, the marriage line has its own importance and this line should be studied with enough care.

◆◆

The Secondary (Unimportant) Lines

The palm has many such lines which are not principal lines but the importance of which is not altogether less in anyway. The study of these lines in itself is quite vital. The lines influence the human life independently or by assisting other important lines. I am hereby dealing briefly with these lines:

1. The Lines of Mars : These lines originate either from the lower region of the Mars or from the initial part of the life line and proceed towards the mount of Venus. Such lines can be more than one or just one. All such lines can be thin, thick, prominent or faint. But one thing is obvious that these lines originate from the mount of Mars and are thus called the lines of Mars.

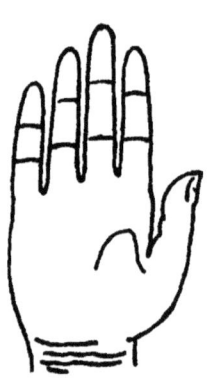

Lines of Mars

These are of two types. The one proceeding along the life line can be called assistant to the life line. Sometimes, such lines proceed parallel to the life line to its very end.

People who have such lines are genius and very intelligent. They are gifted with special powers to think and understand. Whatever decision they once take in their lives, they adhere to it to its end. Such people are trustworthy.

Such people proceed in their lives with a certain aim and do not rest till they have achieved their objective. Physically they are robust and have a very impressive personality. They are not angry by nature.

The second type of lines of Mars are those which do not proceed along the life line, instead they reach the mount of Venus directly. People having this type of lines of Mars are careless in their lives.

They are irritating by nature and can do anything when in rage. They keep company of low-grade people.

If some lines, emitting out of the lines of Mars, move upwards, then those people have many desires in their lives and they leave no stone unturned to get them fulfilled. If such lines meet the fate line then the incumbent will soon have a rise of fate. If these lines join the heart line then the incumbent becomes very sensitive and sentimental.

If such lines of Mars proceeding further cut the fate line or the line of Sun, then the person faces more than necessary obstructions and difficulties in his life. If these lines come in contact with the fate line then the person is considered unlucky. If these lines of Mars touch the line of marriage, then his married life gets spoiled.

If the line of Mars is strong, prominent, inset in the palm and is dual, then certainly the person is either a dacoit or a murderer. But if the line is not dual then the person is able to reach a very high office in military.

2. The Ring of Jupiter or the Ring of Solomon : The line which encircles the root of the index finger—the one which is in semicircle and which encircles the mount of Jupiter, the one end of which goes outside the palm and the other end of which lies between the index finger and the finger of Saturn. Such a ring is called the Ring of the Jupiter or the Ring of Solomon.

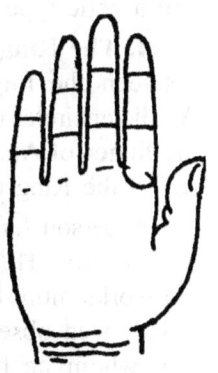

Ring of Jupiter

The person having such a ring is quite sober and generous. He is mostly ambitious. He achieves great success in the field of education. He has one shortcoming. He keeps an air of wealth around him. He also likes useless pomp and show. Such persons try to get maximum benefit from minimum labour but they fail in their efforts. It leads to frustration in their later life.

3. The Ring of Saturn : When a ring-like line encircles the mount of Saturn, the one end of which is between the index finger and the finger of Saturn and the other end lies between the finger of Saturn and the finger of Apollo, it is called the ring of Saturn.

Socially speaking, such a ring is not considered benevolent because a person having such a ring becomes an ascetic and likes loneliness. Such a person relinquishes the attachments and pleasures of this world and tries to improve his next world.

Such persons are found to have achieved success in the field of perfecting charms. If any of the lines of the ring of Saturn does not touch the line of fate then the person achieves success in his aims. But if any of the lines of the ring of Saturn touches the line of the fate, then the concerned persons become a householder many times and an ascetic many times. Such a person fails to get success in his aims. All his tasks remain incomplete or disorderly. He is a slave of sensual pleasures. Sometimes, such persons commit suicide due to self-negation.

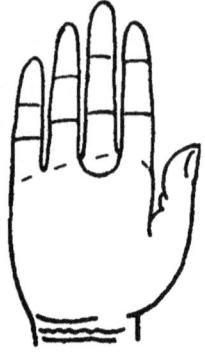
Ring of Saturn

Persons having such a ring are mostly frustrated. They do not get any sort of happiness in their lives. They are thoughtful, lonely and ascetic type persons.

4. The Ring of Sun : If any line originating between the finger of Saturn and the finger of Apollo encircles the mount of Sun and ends between the finger of Apollo and the little finger then it is called the Ring of Sun.

A person having a Ring of Sun leads a very ordinary life. He faces repeated failures in his life. He works more but does not get any credit for it. It has been observed that they certainly discredit him whom he has helped or benefitted. Such a ring converts the benefits of the mount of Sun into losses.

Ring of Sun

Such a person is wise and holds a good moral character, yet he gets discredit and is blamed in social life. Such persons remain frustrated from their lives.

5. The Ring of Venus : If any line originates between the Index finger and the finger of Saturn and passes encircling the mount of Sun and the mount of Saturn ending in between the little finger and the finger of Apollo, then such a ring is called the Ring of Venus.

Those who have this ring are found to be weak and full of troubles. Persons having such rings have diseases of the nervous system. They are also very materalistic in outlook. They have many mental worries and never get peace of mind in their lives.

If this ring is wider enough then such a person spends all the deposited wealth of his ancestors. Such persons are very quick in love affairs and like to have affairs with other women. They suffer from loss of reputation in their lives many times.

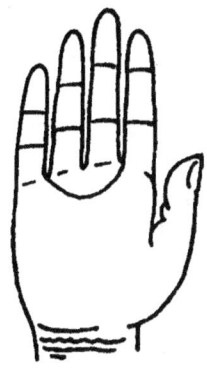

Ring of Venus

If the line of Venus is thin and clear, then such a man is very adjusting and understanding. Such persons are expert in conversation and influence others with their conversation.

If a person has many Venus rings then he has illicit relationship with many women. In the same way, if a woman has many such rings, then she has illicit relationship with many men.

If the ring of Venus breaks in the course, the person has illegitimate relationship with a woman of lower caste but such a person feels sorry for his such evil acts.

If any line coming out of the ring of Venus cuts the marriage line then the incumbent does not get the happiness out of wedlock. Sometimes such persons do not get married. If the ring of Venus proceeding further crosses the fate line then the incumbent becomes unfortunate. He is devoid of any happiness of life.

A person who has a clear mount of Moon and a clear, deep and good ring of Venus, becomes a writer of literature pertaining to youth.

If there is sign of an island on the ring of Venus, then that person is killed due to the conspiracy of his beloved.

If a person has a long thumb and has the ring of Venus then such a man becomes a poet but such persons do not rise much in their lives.

Persons having the ring of Venus are mysterious. They have love for literature and are practical-minded.

If the Sun line lengthens and crosses the ring of Venus, then such persons are libertine. If one part of the ring of Venus goes to the mount of Mercury, then the incumbent gets success through business. If the ring of Venus is cut by many small lines then the person is very lascivious. Careful study of the ring of Venus is very important for a palmist.

6. The Line of Moon or the Line of Luna : This line is considered very important in a person's palm. It is also called the *line of intuition*. This line starts from the wrist joint or from the mount of Luna and reaches the regions of Mercury in the form of a bow.

Those who have this line reach to the height of their career, though they are born in very ordinary families. Sometimes they become presidents or commanders-in-chief. Such persons occupy the posts of importance in a nation.

Moon Line

Such persons have dangers from a voyage. Sometimes, while swimming they face death-like difficulty. They are simple, gentle and sober type. Their personality is captivating and they even have the capacity to enchant their enemies. Such persons always help others and if someone ever does them any good, they remain grateful to him forever.

Such persons give right guidance and direction to the country and the society at the time of crisis.

7. The Influencing Lines : Persons who have these influencing lines are helped a lot in their rising. The lines may start from anywhere and touch the mounts of Venus or Sun or Jupiter or Mercury or Saturn.

Those lines which are strong touch the mounts of Mercury or Sun or Saturn and Jupiter but those which are weak, can't reach.

Such lines help in the advancement of an individual but if such lines cross the fate line, the man becomes unfortunate. Similarly, if any influencing line crosses the health line then the person has very weak health. If any influencing line crosses the head line of a person, then surely the person becomes a lunatic in his life.

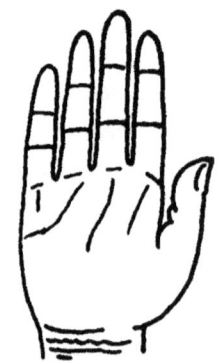
Influencing Line

But if any influencing line joins the fate line of a person, then the person's fate smiles on him. Such a person gets sudden wealth and gets success in his life with the help of his personality.

If some influencing lines originate from the region of the Moon then such a person becomes a poet or a sensitive man or a painter or a lover of beauty. Such person has a very enchanting personality and he gets fame in his life.

If some influencing lines start from the mount of Venus, then such a person will be a cheat, a bunk and a licentious man. Influencing lines starting from the line of the Mars make a man courageous.

8. The Line of Education : This line originates between the finger of Saturn and the finger of Apollo. It proceeds ahead leaning over the region of the Sun. Those who have this line get full scccess in the field of education.

Sometimes it has been found that persons who have this line do not get higher education, yet they are very wise and intelligent. They are honoured in the civilized society and due to their wisdom, they are able to get success in their lives.

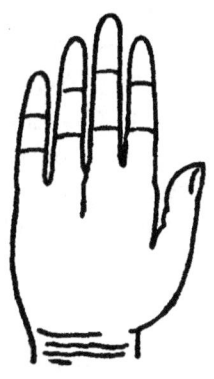
Education Line

9. The Lines of Science : Just as there are lines of issues adjacent to the mount of Mercury, similarly, there are the lines of science. If there are five perpendicular lines on the mount of Mercury, then they are called the lines of science. Those who have these lines, either they are themselves very famous scientists or they earn wealth, fame and honour by writing scientific books. Such persons are clever, laborious and take quick decisions.

10. The Lines of Travelling : Travelling lines are those which compel a person to go on travels and lead him to success by means of travelling.

Science Line

If any line starts from the region of the Mars and meets the life line and if the person has white half-moon on the nail of the finger of Saturn, then the person undertakes many travels in his life.

If a person has half-moon on the nail of the finger of Saturn and it continues there for three months, along with it, a line starting from the region of Pluto goes to the mount of Sun, then certainly that man goes abroad.

If any line starting from the mount of Venus goes to the mount of Moon in the shape of a bow and the finger of Saturn has white half-moon, then that person goes abroad in a ship.

If two equally long lines go upward on the mount of Moon, then that person certainly goes on travels.

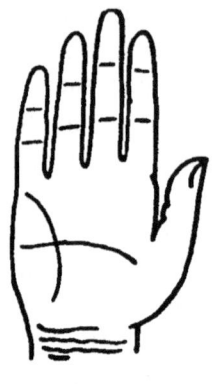

Lines of Travelling

If two parallel lines move upward from the regions of Venus and Harshal, then surely that man goes on travels.

11. The Lines of Brothers and Sisters : These lines start from the mount of Venus and go towards the region of Mars. As many are these lines, so many will be brothers and sisters to a person. If these lines are clear, deep and faultless, then the health of the brothers and sisters will be good. If these lines are weak and broken, then the health of brothers and sisters will also be weak.

Out of these, the lines which are wide and deep are indicative of the number of brothers, the narrow lines indicate the number of sisters.

The one which breaks on the way or which is cut into pieces, indicates that the brother or sister will die in the life-time of a person.

If a person does not have these lines then that person has neither a brother nor a sister.

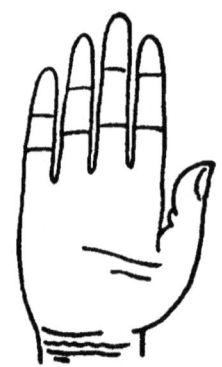

Brothers-Sisters Lines

12. The Lines of Friends : There are some perpendicular lines on the phalanges of the fingers. These are indicative of friends. If there are no perpendicular lines on the phalanges of fingers, then it should be assumed that the person loves loneliness and has practically no support from friends.

The prominence and faultlessness of these lines is related to the sincerty of friends. Contrary to it, if these lines are weak then the person does not get cooperation from friends. Instead his friends cheat him.

Horizontal lines on the phalanges of fingers indicate foes. If these lines are prominent and clear then the foes will be strong. Contrary to it, if these lines are weak, he will be able to dominate his foes.

If the index finger has perpendicular line, it indicates friends in service. In the same way, the horizontal lines on the index finger indicate foes in service.

Perpendicular lines on the finger of Saturn indicate artist friends and the horizontal lines indicate faithless friends.

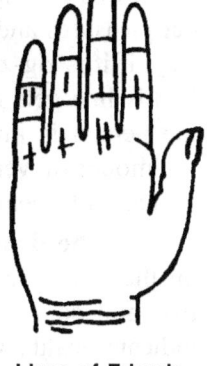

Lines of Friends

Perpendicular lines on the finger of Apollo indicate friendship with high standard friends whereas the horizontal lines indicate high official enemy.

Perpendicular lines on the little finger indicate that the friends will be from business class, whereas horizontal lines indicate that the business class friends will cheat.

If the perpendicular lines cross the sections and go ahead then such friends try to cheat. These lines should be studied carefully.

13. The Casual Lines : These lines crop up casually to show their effect. When their related work ends, then these lines disappear. These can crop up or disappear anywhere on the palm.

They increase the influence of the line parallel to which they move. Contrary to it, if these casual lines cross any line, they minimise the good effect of that line.

A palmist should study these lines also very carefully.

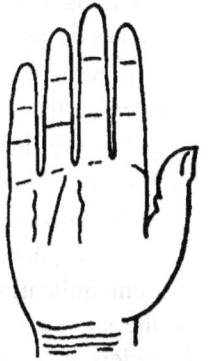

14. The Suman Line or Via Lasciva : This line appears to start from the Dragon's Tail and reaches the areas of the Mercury. If this line touches

Casual Lines

the health line then the incumbent has to suffer great diseases, but if it moves parallel to the health line, the incumbent remains healthy.

If this line reaches the areas of Mercury without crossing any other line, then that person becomes respectable in the country and reaches heights in diplomatic affairs.

If this line is chained, then the person doesn't get pleasures and peace in the family. In the same way, if it is zig-zag, then he suffers from jaundice. If this line gets divided into two at the end, then the person is impotent. If one end of it reaches the mount of Venus, then the person is extremely sexual and licentious.

15. The Bracelets : The three horizontal lines on the wrist are called the Bracelets. Some have two and some have four bracelets. These lines indicate health, wealth, honour and respect.

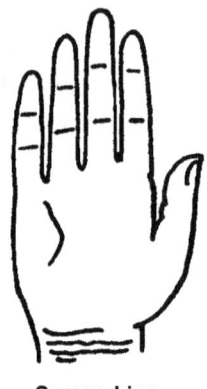
Suman Line

If a line starting from the wrist goes up, then the person gets all his wishes fulfilled in his life time. If any line starting from the wrist leads to the mount of Moon, then the person goes abroad many times.

According to Palmistry, if there are four bracelets, then he lives upto 100 years. One who has three such lines, lives till 75 years of age, one who has two, lives upto the age of 50 and one having only one line on the wrist lives upto 25 years of age.

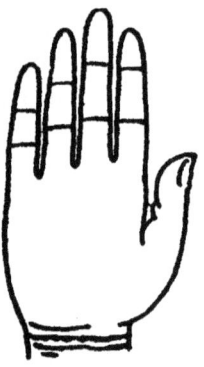
Bracelets

If these lines are broken and in pieces, then the person faces difficulties. Contrary to it, if these lines are faultless and prominent, then the person has better chances of rise of fate.

If the bracelets are chained, then there are continuous difficulties faced by a person. A sign of barley on them indicates good fortune; a point indicates that the persons will have to suffer from diseases of the stomach, an island indicates accidents in his life and chained bracelets indicate hard luck for a person.

If two bracelets meet each other, the person may suffer loss of a limb in an accident. If the lines are bluish, then he remains ill for the whole of his life. Yellow lines indicate that he will have to suffer due to untrustworthiness of others. In fact, the more prominent and faultless the bracelets are, the better it is for the person.

16. The Lines of Venus : The perpendicular and horizontal lines found on the mount of Venus are called the *lines of Venus*. It is to be remembered in this connection that those lines which start from the thumb and move towards the health line, are to be called the lines of Venus.

If these lines are deep, clear and faultless, then they help in giving positive results. Contrary to it, if these lines are broken, weak and indifferent, then the person has to face many difficulties in his life. His rise of fate is delayed and he faces blame in the society.

Lines of Venus

17. The Ring of Mercury : If any line originates between the finger of Apollo and the little finger and encircling the mount of Mercury goes outside the palm, then the formation of such a ring is called the *Ring of Mercury*.

Such a ring of Mercury weakens the characteristics of Mercury. He faces many difficulties in the field of education in his boyhood days. During youth, he does not enjoy the physical pleasures and his life ahead is always a bed of thorns.

Ring of Mercury

18. The Mysterious Cross : This cross lies between the heart line and the head line. It is called the *mysterious cross*. A person who has this cross is prosperous from the scientific point of view.

If this cross is below the mount of Jupiter, then the person certainly achieves his aim. If it is below the mount of Saturn, then the person gets fame in the field of literature. If this cross is near the mount of Moon the person becomes a poet, whichever mount is influenced by this cross, its characteristics increase.

19. The Lines of Accident : The lines which originate from the mount of Saturn and cross the head line are called the lines of accident.

Mysterious Cross

The sign of cross indicates accident. If the

cross is on the mount of Jupiter, then it gives good results and improves the fate. On the mount of Saturn, a cross indicates death in an accident. If there is a cross on the mount of Mars, the person dies in a battlefield. If there is a cross on the mount of Sun, then he will die because of unfaithfulness. Cross on the mount of Mercury indicates that the incumbent will die in an accident due to a fast speeding vehicle. A cross on the mount of Moon indicates that the person will die due to drowning. If there is a cross on the head line then the person becomes insane and a cross on the heart line indicates that the person will lead a widowed life.

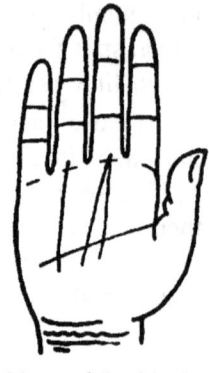
Lines of Accident

Traingle

20. The Triangle : The traingle formed by the meeting of life line, heart line and the line of Mars, in the palm, indicates unparalleled wealth to a person. A person having this triangle gets sudden wealth.

21. Rectangle : If the head line and heart line construct a rectangle in the palm then such person is kind and wise. He also gets honour and respect from the society.

I have briefly dealt with the smaller lines in the palm. Every small line found in the palm is significant so a palmist should never think any line useless, instead, he should study it minutely. By doing so, he will certainly achieve his objectives.

◆◆

Rectangle

Other Signs in the Hand

In the previous chapter, we have dealt with the other lines of the hand but besides these lines, there are other signs also, the study of which is vital for human beings. The other significant signs found in the palm are eight in all. They are:

1. Triangles
2. Crosses
3. Points
4. Circles
5. Islands
6. Squares
7. Nets and
8. Stars

Now I am dealing briefly with each of them.

1. The Triangles : If three lines coming from three different directions join in the palm, a triangle is formed. The triangle can be big or small. One can see such triangles in the palm at different places.

1. The triangle formed by clear, flawless and deep lines is considered benevolent.
2. The size of the triangle is directly related to good results and good fortune. If the triangle is big, its benefits and good luck are also enormous.
3. Triangle found in the mid-palm indicates that the person is very lucky, theist and progressive. His physical and mental activities are pious. Such a person is calm and amiable. He is honoured in the society.

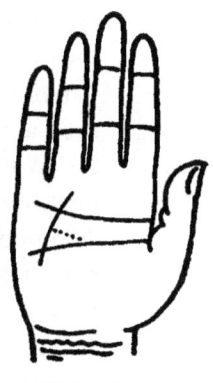
Triangle

4. A big triangle is indicative of large-heartedness of an individual.
5. A narrow and hazy triangle indicates narrow-mindedness of a person.
6. If in the palm of a person, there is a smaller triangle inset in a bigger one, then that person certainly gets success in getting a higher post.
7. If there is a triangle on the mount of Venus, then the person is simple, congenial, sentimental, a lover of decent living and is a high standard person.
8. If there is a wayward or faulty triangle in the palm, then the person is licentious and lover of other women. If there is such a triangle in the palm of a woman, then she is certainly a flirt.
9. If there is a triangle on the mount of Mars, then the person is a warrior and exhibits courage and patience in the battlefield. He is decorated with national medals for bravery. But if the triangle on the mount of Mars is faulty then the person is cruel and coward.
10. If a person has a faultless triangle on the Dragon's Head then he acquires a very high post in his youth. He also gets success in the field of politics. But if there are two joined triangles on the Dragon's Head then the person is considered to have ill-luck.
11. If there is a nice triangle on Pluto, then that person's old age is spent joyfully but if there are two joined triangles, then he faces blemishes in his old age.
12. If there is a faultless triangle on the mount of Jupiter, then such a person is cunning, diplomatic and always desires for his own progress. Contrary to it, if the triangle is faulty, then the person is proud and selfish.
13. A faultless triangle on the mount of Saturn indicates that the person is an authority on exorcism and charms. If the triangle is faulty then the person is a great cheat and most unreliable.
14. If there is a triangle on the mount of Sun, then the person is very religious, a benefactor and well-wisher of others but if the triangle is faulty, he is criticised by the society.

He does not get success in life and there are hindrances in the rise of his fate.

15. If there is a triangle in the region of Mars then the person becomes a successful scientist in his life. He also achieves a great success in business. Such persons spread their business.
16. A triangle on the life line indicates longevity for the person.
17. A triangle on head line indicates that the person is very intelligent and will get very good education.
18. If a person has a triangle on the heart line, then his fate rises in the ripe age.
19. A triangle on the health line indicates very decent health.
20. A triangle on the Sun line indicates that the person will get international fame in some particular field.
21. The person who has a triangle on the fate line, is always considered unlucky. Such persons are unsuccessful in their lives.
22. If there is a triangle on the marriage line, then there are many hindrances in his marriage and his married life remains nearly unsuccessful.
23. If a person has a triangle on the Moon line, then he goes abroad many times and achieves success.
24. If a triangle is formed by the life line and the head line, then it is considered auspicious.
25. If a triangle is formed by the health line and the head line, then the person is very intelligent.
26. If a triangle is formed by the health line and the life line, it helps in raising the person to a great height.
27. If there is a protruding triangle in the palm of a person, then he is quarrelsome by nature.
28. If the lines of a triangle are protruding, strong and wide, then the individual takes care of the welfare of others.
29. If the lines of the triangle are quite wide and the person has a strong mount of Mars, then he is sure to move ahead.
30. If there are flat triangles in both the hands of a person, then his life is quite unimportant.

31. If the lines are deep and narrow, then he certainly gets success in his life.
32. If the lines of the triangle are faint and broken, then the person is selfish and materialistic more than enough.
33. If some assisting lines proceed upwards from the triangle, then the person gets success after many hindrances.
34. If the inside of the triangle is wide, then the person is lazy.
35. If the health line is prominent and the triangle is also big, then it indicates longevity for the individual.
36. If there is a cross over the triangle, then the person faces many accidents in his life.
37. If a person has long fingers and there is a cross inside the triangle, then he worries others.
38. If there is a cross under the triangle then the person becomes very important in his life.
39. If there is a cross in the middle of the triangle and a star near the health line, then the person becomes blind.
40. If there is a sign of star inside the triangle, then the person earns ill-fame in a love affair.
41. If there is a circle inside the triangle, then he is cheated by his beloved.
42. A prominent, strong and big triangle is considered very favourable for the rise of an individual from all points of view.

2. Crosses : A cross is formed when a vertical line meets a horizontal line forming a 'plus' or an 'into' sign. This sign is auspicious only on the mount of Jupiter, otherwise a cross never provides a favourable result.

1. If there is a cross over the region of Jupiter, then the man leads a happy and joyful life. He does work after a lot of consideration. His wife is educated. He gets wealth from his in-laws. His domestic life is happy and peaceful.

Crosses

2. If there is a cross on the mount of Saturn, the incumbent gets bodily injuries in fights and quarrels. Such a man has a premature death.
3. If there is a cross on the region of Sun, the person faces too much ill-fame from the society. He faces difficulties in business and his fortune never assists him in his life.
4. A cross on Mercury indicates that the person is a great cheat, imposter and crafty. Such a person can never be believed upon.
5. If a person has a cross on the region of Moon, he dies by drowning or he suffers from mental ailments throughout his life.
6. If there is a cross on the region of Harshal, then the person is lazy and coward. He is always afraid of his foes.
7. A cross on the Dragon's tail indicates that the person was brought up in misery and he could be given no proper education.
8. If there is a cross on the region of Venus, then the person has had unsuccessful love affair and got ill-fame for it. Such persons engage themselves in notorious jobs.
9. A cross mark on the mount of Mars indicates that the person will suffer imprisonment. Such a person is quarrelsome and he commits suicide to end his own life.
10. If there is a cross on the Dragon's Head, the person spends his youth in misery and he suffers from small pox.
11. If there is a sign of cross on any other mount, excepting that of Jupiter, then the mounts indicate opposite results.
12. If there is a cross on the line of travelling, then the person dies suddenly while on a travel.
13. If there is a cross mark on the line of marriage, then the person does not get married. If he gets married, his domestic life becomes miserable.
14. A cross mark on the line of issues indicates issuelessness.
15. A sign of cross on the health line is responsible for the ill-health of an individual.
16. If there is a mark of cross on the fate line, then the person is obliged to lead a very ordinary life.

17. A cross mark on the Sun line indicates hindrances in the progress of an individual.
18. If there is a mark of cross on the heart line, then the person suffers from heart attack. He also remains weak.
19. If there is a cross mark on the head line, then the person remains afflicted with mental diseases and becomes insane in the end.
20. If there is a cross mark on the life line, then the person suffers death-like misery at that particular age.
21. Any sort of cross, whether small or big, wide or narrow is regarded as detrimental.

3. Points : Points also wield great significance in the palm. White points are always indicative of progress. The red-coloured points indicate diseases. Yellow-coloured points indicate anaemic body conditions. If there are black-coloured points, the person gets wealth. The black-coloured points are called 'Tils'. In the following lines, I am describing the effect of having 'Tils' or black-coloured points in the palm.

Points

1. If the black point (Til) is in the palm and it encloses in the closed fist, then such a person does not lack wealth.
2. If the black point does not enclose in the closed fist but remains outside then the person has wealth but he cannot accumulate it. He spends it as it comes.
3. If there is black point on the mount of Jupiter, then he faces hindrances in his marriage. He suffers from bad name in a love affair in the society. Such a person cannot get success in life.
4. If there is a black point in the region of Saturn, then he faces notoriety in love affairs. His domestic life becomes miserable and either the husband or the wife commits suicide by burning oneself in fire.
5. If there is a black point on the mount of Sun, then the person receives a great shock to his honour and he is compelled to do mean works in the society.

6. If there is a black point on the area of Mercury, then the person is cunning and cheat. Such a person suffers loss in business.
7. A black point on the area of Moon indicates undue delay in a person's marriage. He also faces many accidents in water.
8. If there is a black point on the area of Harshal, then one of the limbs of the person is cut by a weapon.
9. A black point on the area of Dragon's tail makes the incumbent's childhood miserable.
10. If there is a black point on the area of Venus, then the person is lascivious and his secret organs suffer from a certain disease.
11. A black point on the life line indicates that the person will suffer from T.B. for a long time.
12. A black point on the regions of Dragon's head indicates economic loss in a person's youth.
13. If there is a black point on the head line of an individual, then he gets serious head injury and suffers from mental diseases.
14. If there is a black point on the heart line, then the person is weak-hearted.
15. A black point on the Sun line indicates perpetual hindrances in the progress of an individual.
16. If there is a black point on the fate line of a person, then his whole life remains unfortunate.
17. A black point on the health line makes a person weak throughout his life.
18. A black point on the marriage line indicates hindrances in marriage.
19. If there is a black point on the line of Mars, then the person is a coward and weak-hearted individual.
20. A black point on the line of Moon hampers progress of an individual.
21. If there is a black point on the line of travelling, then the person dies while on travel.
22. A black point on the finger of Apollo indicates failure in business.

23. If there is a black point on the little finger, then the person suffers loss in business and cannot extend his business.
24. A black point on the finger of Saturn indicates hindrances in one's fate. He has to wander about for the rise of his fate.
25. If there is a black point on the index finger, then the person has to resign from service. He also faces ill-fame.

4. Circles : The small round rings found in the palm are known as *circles or the Suns*.

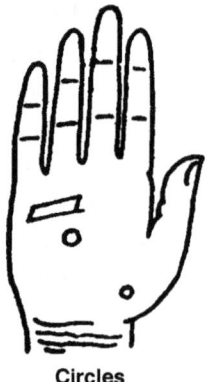

Circles

1. If there is a circle on the mount of Jupiter in the palm, then the person is influential. He certainly gets a higher post by his efforts. Such a person also gets wealth from his in-laws.
2. If there is a circle on the mount of Saturn, then the incumbent gets sudden wealth and also gets wealth through lottery, speculation or gambling.
3. If there is a circle on the mount of Sun, then the person is of high thinking and has pure and honest thoughts. He becomes famous in the world.
4. A circle on the mount of Mercury provides great success in business. Such a person has a life full of dalliance and enjoyment.
5. A circle on the mount of Harshal makes a person weak and lazy.
6. If there is a circle on the mount of Moon, the person has then weak health and he dies by drowning.
7. If there is a circle on the mount of Venus, then the person engages himself in amorous dalliance and enjoyments. Some-times such persons are impotent.
8. The presence of a circle on the region of Mars makes a person weak-hearted.
9. If there is a circle on the life line then his eyes are weak.
10. A circle on the head line indicates mental diseases.
11. A circle on the heart line indicates heart disease for the incumbent.

12. A circle on the Sun line indicates extraordinary success for the individual. He is quite satisfied materially,
13. If there is a circle on the fate line then it indicates ill-fortune for the person. He faces difficulties throughout his life.
14. If there is a circle on the line of travelling then he faces death-like difficulties in travelling.

5. Islands : This sign can be found anywhere on the palm. Wherever it is found, it reduces the effect of the region.

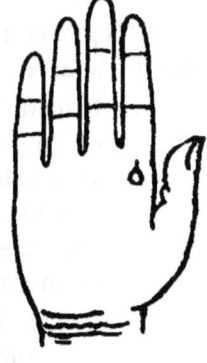

Islands

1. If there is a sign of island on the mount of Jupiter, then the person lacks self-confidence and he has doubt about himself.
2. An island on the mount of Saturn provides difficulties to an individual often and on.
3. If there is an island on the mount of Sun, then the person leads a life full of frustration. He becomes irritating by nature.
4. An island on the mount of Mercury indicates loss in matters concerning business or science. Such persons face ill-fame in the society.
5. If there is an island on the mount of Moon then the person is cruel and tyrant by nature.
6. An island on the mount of Venus is considered detrimental for the family life of a person. He faces all round frustration in his life.
7. If there is an island on the life line then the person is considered sexually weak.
8. An island on the head line gives mental diseases to a person.
9. If there is an island on the heart line then it gives heart trouble to a person throughout his life.
10. If there is an island on the Sun line then he faces notoriety in his life many times.
11. An island on the fate line indicates ill-fortune. Such a person faces more than enough difficulties in his life.
12. If there is an island on the line of travelling then that person

dies while travelling.

13. An island on the mount of Moon makes a person dull.
14. If there is an island on the line of marriage then the person suffers the loss of his or her living partner.
15. If there is an island on the line of health then the person has to withstand many diseases in his span of life.

6. Squares : The area or a place surrounded by four lines is called a square.

1. If there is a sign of square on the mount of Jupiter, then the person becomes a successful administrator. His fame and honour spread throughout the world. He rises to a very high post though he is born in an ordinary family.
2. If there is a sign of square on the mount of Saturn, then the person surprisingly escapes death repeatedly.
3. If the sign of square is on the region of Sun, then the person leads a very high standard of life regarding his honour, respect, post and fame. The fame of his works spreads all over.
4. If there is a square on the mount of Mercury, he escapes imprisonment.
5. A square mark on the mount of Moon increases the power of imagination of a person. Such a person is sober and kind. He keeps patience even in opposing circumstances.
6. If there is a mark of square on the Dragon's Tail, then such a person should expect early rise of fortune. He spends a jolly good time in his youth.
7. If there is a square mark on the mount of Venus, then the person takes caution in love affairs and thus escapes scandals.
8. If there is a square on the mount of Mars, one is able to contain his anger. He gets angry rarely in his life.
9. A sign of square on the line of travelling denotes that the incumbent will go on journey several times and that he will earn wealth from his travels.
10. A sign of square on the line of Moon assists a person in

Squares

all sorts of progress.

11. If there is a sign of square on the marriage line then the person has an educated, beautiful and amiable wife. He also gets wealth from his in-laws.
12. If there is a sign of square on the health line then the personality of the person becomes fascinating. His health remains sound throughout his life.
13. If there is a square mark on the fate line then the fate of the person rises at an early age.
14. A mark of square on the line of Sun indicates honour, respect, high post and fame for the incumbent throughout his life.
15. If there is a sign of square on the heart line then his family life is full of happiness. Such a person is kind and generous by heart.
16. A sign of square on the head line indicates that the person will always have balance of mind and he remains active throughout his life.
17. If there is a square mark on the life line then the person enjoys longevity.
18. If there is a square mark on the Dragon's Head, then the incumbent spends enough time in the company of sages in forests.

In nutshell, the square mark in the palm at any place is considered auspicious.

7. Nets : The horizontal lines on the vertical lines form a sort of net. It is available anywhere in the palm. The results of such nets are as follows:

1. If there is a net on the region of Jupiter, then such a person is cruel, tyrant, selfish and proud.
2. If there is a net on the mount of Saturn, then the person is lazy. He suffers ill-fame due to his miserly habits.
3. If the net is on the mount of Sun, then the incumbent has to face ill-fame repeatedly.

Nets

4. If the net is on the mount of Mercury, then the person repents over his own doings and faces difficulties.
5. If there is a net on the region of Harshal, then the person surely commits a murder and has to suffer imprisonment.
6. If there is a net on the mount of Moon, then the person is fickle-minded and remains dissatisfied.
7. If there is a net on the Dragon's Tail, then the person remains perturbed throughout his life due to illnesses.
8. If there is net mark on the mount of Venus, then that person indulges in excessive dalliance and is licentious. He has no place whatsoever in the society.
9. If there is a net on the region of Mars, then the person remains impatient mentally throughout his life.
10. A net mark on the region of Dragon's Head indicates unavoidable unfortunate life for the incumbent.
11. If there is a net mark on the bracelets, then the incumbent faces a great downfall.
12. Nowhere in the palm is the sign of net considered favourable.

8. Stars : If we see minutely in the palm, we find stars at many places. Their results differ with their different places.

1. If there is a mark of star on the mount of Jupiter, then that person certainly achieves full success in his life. He does not lack wealth, respect, honour and high post in his life. He always ascends to progress and achieves a respectable post and a great success in the society.
2. If there is a sign of star on the mount of Saturn, then such a person gets rapid rise in fortune. He moves ahead towards his aim and gets fame and respect in his life.
3. If there is a star mark on the mount of Sun, then such a person gets full benefit of wealth in his life. Materially, he does not lack anything in his life. He also remains healthy— physically and mentally.

Star

4. If there is a star mark on the mount of Mercury, then such a person becomes a successful businessman and a top planner. Such a person can also be a successful poet and writer.
5. If there is a mark of star on the Dragon's Tail, then that person's childhood is spent very happily and he does not need any material thing in his life.
6. If there is a star on the mount of Venus, then that person indulges in too much sexual activities. He has illicit relationship with other women as well. His wife remains very healthy and beautiful.
7. A star mark on the mount of Mars indicates that the person is courageous and patient. He gets national honour for his valour in war.
8. If there is a mark of star on the Dragon's Head, then his fortune always favours him. He gets full fame and honour in his life.
9. A star mark on the line of travelling shows that the person will die away from his house at a place of pilgrimage.
10. If there is a mark of star on the line of Moon, then that person suffers from stomach ailments and remains sick one way or the other.
11. If there is a mark of star on the line of Mars, then that person gets killed.
12. If there is a mark of star on the line of marriage, then that person faces many obstructions in his marriage and his family life cannot be termed as a happy one.
13. If there is a mark of star on the health line, then that person remains weak in health throughout his life and dies in miserable circumstances.
14. If there is a star on the Sun line, then the person gets extraordinary success in business and gets many fortunate moments to acquire wealth in his life.
15. If there is a star on the heart line, then he suffers from diseases related to heart.
16. If there is a sign of star on the head line, then the person suffers from diseases of the nerves for the whole of his

life.
17. If a person has a mark of star on the life line, he dies suddenly in his youth.
18. If a person has a sign of star on the thumb, he is laborious, patient and successful.
19. A sign of star on the index finger is always quite auspicious.
20. Marks of stars on the finger of Saturn and other fingers make their respective stars stronger.

Hence, it is necessary to study a mark of star on the hand with utmost caution. These marks assist in the making of a personality and are also important in forecasting.

Determining the Time

In the previous chapters, I have dealt with certain facts about lines of the palm along with it, I have also stated about the assisting lines and signs or marks found on a hand. But with this, a natural question arises that, 'when will a certain event happen in the life of a man?' To know and understand it is also very necessary.

In the life of a person, there are many perplexing questions—When will the fortune smile? How will it take place? Will it take place in this country or in a foreign country? When will one go abroad? When will one get a job? When will there be stability in the business? How much will one gain in business and when? What things or what works will give profit in the business? When will there be increase in income? When will one get promotion in the service? How much happiness will one get from one's children? When will one get married? and so on. These are the problems which crowd up in the mind of a person. For all these, it is therefore, very necessary to understand the process of determining time so that the foretelling may be clear and accurate.

In the previous pages, I have provided information regarding the heart line, the fate line, the health line, the head line and the life line. The study of life line is the most necessary.

As already stated earlier that the line which originates between the thumb and the index finger, moves circling the mount of Venus and reaches the bracelets is called the life line.

Firstly, for practice, one has to measure the life line with a thread from its starting point to the first line of the wrist. Considering the total length of the thread as a hundred years, it is to be divided into ten equal parts. Now one part will be equivalent to a period of ten years. This also is to be further divided into ten equal parts, Now each smaller part will be equivalent to a period of one year. After some practice, one will be able to assess correctly by just seeing the hand that how many years are represented by the life line of a person. If the life line ends abruptly then at that particular period one should assume that it is the end of one's life. It will definitely tell one's age. Wherever one finds a cross on the life line or it gets fade, then at that age, one suffers from a serious disease or may suffer from death-like misery. This should be understood.

All the events are indicated only by the life line in the hand. From a point on other lines, if one draws a straight line towards the life line, then the point where it touches the life line indicates the year in which a certain event will take place. To make it concrete, if there is a cut in the fate line at a certain point, then a straight line drawn from the cut towards the life line touches the life line at the age of 42. Thus we conclude that the individual will have a hurdle in his fortune at the age of 42 and he may have to face a big difficulty in his fate at that age.

In the same way, results of other lines can be calculated and the time of the occurrence of the events may also be known.

One should try this gradually. After such practice, just a view of the palm will tell one the related incident and its time.

A successful fortune-teller and an expert palmist will be recognized only when he is able to tell the correct time of an event and for that purpose, I have clarified the above point.

◆◆

Procedure of Taking Hand-prints

My centre receives hundreds of letters from people desirous of knowing their future through the study of hand-prints. The services of this centre are available to the people of this country and also to those living in foreign countries and it is a matter of great happiness that people have certainly availed the opportunity so offered to them by my centre. Though studying hands personally is always most preferable to studying the hand-prints because of the obvious reason that one can see the protrusion of the mounts only when shown personally and also that even the smallest lines can also be studied when shown the hand personally. But this facility is not available for all. Those who are far away and those who live in foreign countries, for them hand-print is the only medium through which they can know their future.

So far as my experience goes, only a good camera can take an accurate photograph of the hand and in it the bulging of the mounts of different planets can be seen. Besides, even the camera and all the lines can be seen in the photograph which help in forecasting correctly. In my opinion, those who want accurate forecasting should send photographs of their hands.

Where the facility of taking photographs is not available, they can send their hand-prints also but while doing so, they should take the following precautions:

1. The paper should be white and not rough. It should neither be thin nor be very smooth. It should not absorb ink.
2. While taking the print on the paper, it should be seen that the paper is quite sufficient in length and breadth. No portion of the hand should be kept out of the paper.
3. Before taking print, the hand should be washed with soap and there should be no ring on the finger.

Methods

In the following lines, I am introducing three or four methods of taking hand-prints clearly:

1. Taking Prints Through Smoke : Take a white (a bit hard) paper. It should be big enough to have space all around even after placing the full hand on it. Take a tablet of camphor in a utensil and ignite the tablet so that it burns and emits smoke. Put the paper over the utensil, taking care that it does not burn but only blackens. Move the paper to and fro to have good blackening. Let a thick coat of black smoke stick to the paper. The black coating should be uniform on the paper. If one tablet burns up, then add another to it. One should keep at least 10 or 12 camphor tablets at hand.

When the rear portion of the paper is completely blackened then put it on a flat and smooth table. There should be no cloth over the table. The surface of the table should be smooth and hard. The black part of the paper should remain upwards.

Now spread your hand and put it over the paper. Keep the fact in view that the impression of all the fingers of your hand and even the bracelets is on the paper. Now press your hand so that the impression of all the lines is transferred to the paper.

Now remove your hand straight off. You will see that the impression of even the smallest lines of your hand has been imprinted on the paper. If you can put a small handkerchief under the paper in its centre so that your palm comes just over it, then the impression recorded will be fool proof.

On a corner of this paper, write your name, address, date of birth and date of taking the hand-print. Put a white paper covering the hand-print so that the impressions do not mix up. Now fold it carefully and send it to a palmist for his study and get your forecast.

2. Taking Hand-print with the Help of Press Ink : In a printing press, there is big roller containing ink. When the books or materials have been printed, the ink on the roller fades. We should use this faded ink from the roller.

Spread a big white paper on a table then put a handkerchief under the paper. Now put your right hand on the roller and see that the whole of your palm is smeared with ink. When you are sure that the whole of your hand contains ink then put your hand cautiously over the paper and press it. Take the precaution that the centre of the palm is over the handkerchief so that a correct print is available.

When you have fixed your hand on the paper, press the joints with the other hand. Now remove your hand without moving it. You will see that the lines of your hand have been printed on the paper.

In the similar way, take a print of your left hand. Let the ink dry up for a few minutes. When it has dried, write your name, address and date of birth on the paper and send it to the palmist for his predictions.

In my opinion, everyone should send at least three sets of hand-prints so that one may know the handicaps of one hand-print in the other ones.

3. Hand-prints with Ink-pads : The ink pads used for putting rubber stamps are easily available. So one can easily get hand-prints by using ink-pad. The procedure of taking down hand-prints through this method is the same as that of taking down hand-prints through press-ink.

4. Hand-prints Through Photographs : This method is more accurate and authentic. One has to select an expert photographer for it. Care should also be taken that the light is neither too much so as to hide the smaller line of the hand in its brightness nor should it be so less that the smaller lines don't find their impression in the photograph. The photographer should be told beforehand about all this. The photograph should contain the impressions of the whole hand upto the wrist lines. The fingers should be separated while getting the photograph and they should not be attached or joined with each other.

The quality of the paper of the photograph should be very good. There can be one photograph of both the hands. It should not, however, be smaller than a post-card-sized photo.

By employing any of the above methods, an individual can get the hand-prints of his/her hands. These hand-prints can be sent to any fortune-teller, so that he may find out one's future accurately.

◆◆

The Goddess Panchanguli

In the previous chapter, I have given a detailed account of the different lines and mounts found in the hand but I have not been able to give any information regarding the Goddess Panchanguli. In this chapter, I am giving in brief the information regarding it. One who wants to study in detail in this regard, should read my book *Palmistry and the Devotion to the Panchanguli*.

We get information regarding Panchanguli in many ancient books and it has been described there that one who worships Goddess Panchanguli regularly, becomes a successful fortune-teller very quickly. If he sees the hand of any person, he can presently find the past, the present and the future of that man. He also becomes aware of the minutest mysteries of the life of the man.

It is obvious that the famous western palmist, Cheiro also worshipped Goddess Panchanguli. Cheiro had lived in India for three years and had studied the worshipping of Goddess Panchanguli from an ascetic. He became famous due to this worshipping. I personally feel that the worshipping of Goddess Panchanguli provides a complete knowledge about the lines of the hand to an individual.

In its worshipping, an auspicious time is a must.

The Month

This worshipping can be started in any month but Vaishakh, Kartik, Ashwin and Magh months are considered more auspicious.

The Date

This worshipping can be started on the second, the fifth, the seventh, the eighth, the tenth or the fifteenth day of the bright half of the Moon.

The Day

Sunday, Wednesday, Thursday and Friday are considered the best to start this worshipping.

The Nakshtra

Kritika, Rohini, Poonarvasu, Hast, all the three Uttaras, Anuradha and Shravana Nakshtras are considered favourable for it.

The Lagna

Sthir, Vrish, Singh, Vrishchik and Kumbh.

The Place

Pilgrims' place, confluence of the Ganges and the Yamuna, bank of a river, cave of a mountain and temple of Skandh are auspicious places. But if these places are not easily available, then a lonely room of the house can be used.

The Panchanguli Yantra

In any *Tantra* worship, one needs (if necessary) a *yantra* to be used. To accomplish the worshipping of Panchanguli, one needs a picture of Goddess Panchanguli and consecrated and life-imparted Panchanguli *yantra*. If one contacts our centre, such a *yantra* and picture can be sent to the desirous one.

Articles for Worshipping

Kumkum	*Yagyopaveet*	Black pepper
Abir	Fruit	Honey
Gulal	Coconuts	Ittar (scent)
Mauri	Rice	Deepak
Suparis (nuts)	Almonds	(earthen lamp)
Kesar (saffron)	Cashewnuts	Curd
Batasha	Dried Grapes	Sugar
Milk *Prasad*	*Mishri*	Betels
Camphor	*Incense*	*Bhoja Patra*
Ilaychi	*Loung*	*Peepal* leaves
Ghee	Flowers	Milk (unboiled)
Ganga water	Well-water	Garland of flowers

Some 'Musts' to be Observed

1. No co-habitation and no talks about women.
2. No shaving.

3. Daily worship of *Sandhya* & *Gayatri* should be done.
4. One cannot worship when one is naked, has not bathed, has impious hands and has a cloth over head.
5. One cannot talk with anyone till one finishes one's bead count.
6. If one sneezes or passes out foul air from anus, then one should wash one's hands and touch the holy water to the ears.
7. During the period of prayer, one should abstain from sneezing, laziness, yawning, sleeping, tiredness, fear, impious clothing, talking and being angry.
8. One has to always do the same amount of prayer which one does on the very first day. It should neither be lessened nor be increased.
9. During the period of prayer if one goes to the lavatory for easement, then one should again take a bath and then start praying.

Rules to be Followed During the Period of Prayer

One should observe the following rules during the period of prayer:
1. Sleeping on the ground.
2. Leading a celebate's life.
3. Daily bathing.
4. Keeping silent.
5. Giving alms.
6. Serving the teacher.
7. Not performing sinful deeds.
8. Daily worshipping.
9. Worshipping and praying Gods.
10. Having faith in one's teacher and tutelary deity.
11. Regularity in the prayer.
12. Holiness.

Now in the following pages, I am describing the *Panchanguli Mantra* and the *Kaal Gyan Mantra*. Along with it, I am clarifying the solemn vow *(Sankalpa)*. First of all, the worshipper should make a solemn vow, then he should recite the *Kaal Gyan Mantra* five times and then, before the *Panchanguli yantra*, meditating about the Panchanguli, he should recite the *Panchanguli Mantra* for one hundred and eight times. In the last, he should end his meditation on Panchanguli.

By following this ritual for sixty days, one can accomplish *Panchanguli Sadhana Mantra* or by praying one lakh *Kaal Gyan Mantra*, one can accomplish to know the past and the present of an incumbent.

For the facility of my readers, I am giving here the solemn vow (Sankalpa), the *Panchanguli Dhyan Mantra* and the *Kaal Gyan Mantra* respectively.

संकल्प:

ओ३म् अस्य श्री कस्यचित् सच्चिदानंद रूपस्य ब्रह्मणो निर्वाच्य मायाशक्ति विजृमिता विद्या योगात् कालकर्म स्व-भावाविर्भूत महत्तत्वो दिताहं कारोद्भूत वियदादि पंच महाभूतेन्द्रिय देवता निर्मिते अंडकटाहे चतुर्दश लोकात्मके लीलया तन्मध्यवर्तिनी भगवत: श्री नारायणस्य नाभि कमलोद्भूत सकल लोक पितामहस्य ब्रह्मण: सृष्टिं कुर्वतस्तदुद्धरणाय प्रजापति प्रार्थितस्य श्री सित वाराह वतारेण ध्रिय माणायां यस्यां धरित्र्याम् मुवर्लोक संहितायां सप्तद्वीप मंडितायां क्षीरोदार्धाब्धि द्विग णातीय वलयिकृत लक्ष्योजन विस्तीर्ण जम्बूद्वीपे स्वर्गस्थिता अमराद्या-सा शितवतारे गंगादि सरिद्वि: प्रावित: निखिल जन मुनिकृत निर्वसतिके नैमिषारण्ये कन्या कुमारिके क्षेत्रे पुष्करण्ये श्री मन्मार्तण्डस्य कृपापात्र कालत्रित यज्ञ गर्गवाराह गणितायां संख्याणं श्री ब्रह्मणो द्वितीय पराढ्ढ श्री श्वेत वाराह नाम्नि प्रथम कल्पे, द्वितीये यामे तृतीये मुहूर्त, चतुर्थ युगे, स्वायंभुव: स्वारोचित: उत्तम: तामस: रैवत: चाक्षुसेति षष्मनुनां मतिक्रमोष्यात् क्रम्यमाणे संप्रति वैवस्वत मन्वन्तरे अष्टाविंशति में वर्ष त्रिनवे त्रिग्नेयाते कलियुगे कलि प्रथम चरणे श्री मल्लवणाव्ये उत्तरे तीरे गंगा यमुनयो पश्चिमे तटे शालीवाहन बौद्धावतारे विक्रम भूपकृत: संवत्सरे संवत: .... नाम संवत्सरे (एको न त्रशत्युत्तर द्वि सहस्र में) वर्ष रविनारायण (उत्तरायने) ...कृतौ महामांगल्यप्रद मासोत्तमें मासे शुभ मासे मासे...पक्षे अद्य तिथौ...वाराधिपति श्रीमद् वासरे यथा नक्षत्र योगकारण लग्न एवं ग्रह विशेषण विशिष्टतायां अमुक राशिस्थिते सूर्य अमुक राशिस्थिते चंद्रे अमुक राशिस्थिते देवगुरौ शेषेसु ग्रहेसु यथा-यथा राशिस्थिते सप्तसु एवं ग्रह गुण विशेषण विशिष्टायां शुभपुण्यस्थितौ ...गौत्रस्य श्री (यजमान का नाम) यजमानस्य शरीरे आयु आरोग्य ऐश्वर्यवांछित फल प्राप्तये भार्यादि सर्व सम्पत्ये चिंतितार्थस्य आदि व्याधि जरा मृत्यु भय शोक निवृत्तये परमैश्वर्य संपत्यै

निष्पत्यै अमुक कर्मण पंचांगुलीदेवी पूजन कर्मणी सांगता सिद्ध्यर्थ मम: समस्त कुटुम्बस्य सपरिवारस्य सर्वविघ्नोपशांतये भूत भविष्यत् वर्तमान त्रिविधोत्पात् शांतये भूरिभगयाप्तये पुन: कृतस्य करिष्यमाण: कर्मण: साम्य षुप्त महाफल वाप्तये नित्य नूतन आत्मन: क्षीरोदीपट फुलादिवास सुरभि चन्दन: कर्पूर: कस्तूरी केत्याद्य नेक शरीर भूषण समृद्ध्यर्थ सुवर्ण रौप्य निखिल धातु प्रवाल मौक्तिक माणिक्येन्द्र नीलवज्र वैदूर्यादि नाना रत्न बहुल प्राप्तये यव: ब्रीहि गोधुम तिल माष मुद्गाद्य नेक धन्यानां संतताभि वृद्धये अश्वशाला गौशाला सर्व चतुष्पदशाला प्रपाद्यादिशाला देवपूजास्थान, ब्राह्मण संतर्पणादि सर्वस्यानानाम् सर्व विघ्नोपशांतये मम इह जन्मनि पंचांगुली प्रीति द्वारा सर्वापत्रिवृत्ति पूर्वक: अल्पायु निवृत्ति पूर्वक जन्म लग्नात् वर्ष लग्नात् गोचरात् चतुरस्र अष्ट द्वादश स्थान स्थित सूर्यादि क्रूर ग्रह तज्जनितारिष्ट निवृत्ति पूर्वकं दशा अंतर्दशा उपदशा जनितारिष्ट ज्वर दाह पीड़ा नेत्रकर्णादियो पीड़ा निवृत्ति पूर्वकं अल्पायु निवृत्ति पूर्वकश्चाधि दैविक भौतिक आध्यात्मिक जनित: क्लेश: कायिक वाचिक मानसिक त्रिविधागौध निवृत्ति पूर्वक शरीरारोग्यर्थ धर्मार्थ काम मोक्ष चतुर्विध पुरुषार्थ सिध्यर्थ राजद्वारत: व्यापारतश्च लाभार्थ जयार्थ क्षेमार्थ गतवस्तु प्राप्त्यर्थ स्थिर लक्ष्मी संचितार्थ पुत्र पौत्रा अविच्छिन्न धन समृद्ध्यर्थ वेदशास्त्रोक्त फला वाप्तये कीर्तिलाभ व शत्रु पराजय सद्विष्ट सिद्ध्यर्थ श्री परमेश्वर प्रीत्यर्थ सद्विष्ट सिद्ध्यर्थ यथा संपादित सामग्रयां कलश स्थापन पंचांगुली पूजन महं करिष्ये।

तदंगत्वेन निर्विघ्नतां परि समाप्तयर्थ गणपति पंचौकार वास्तु दिव्यादि चतु: षष्टी योगिनी अजरादि पंचाणत् क्षेत्रपाल सप्त चिरंजीव सप्तवसोद्वारा सप्तऋषि गोर्यादि षोडश मातृका वरुण कलश सूर्यादि नवग्रह तदंगभूत अधिदेवता प्रत्यधि देवता स्थापन पूजनांतर मित्ती पंचांगुली आवाहन कलशस्थापनं तस्योपरि पंचांगुली यहं पूनजं तदंगत्वैनादौ गणपति पूजनं महं करिष्ये।

पंचांगुली ध्यान:

पंचांगुली महादेवी श्री सीमन्धर शासने।
अधिष्ठात्री करस्यासौ शक्ति: श्री त्रिदशेशितु:॥

पंचांगुली मंत्र:

ओ३म् नमो पंचांगुली पंचांगुली परशरी परशरी माता मयंगल वशीकरणी लोहमय दंडमणिनी चौंसठ काम विहंडनी रणमध्ये राउलमध्ये शत्रु मध्ये दीवानमध्ये भूतमध्ये पिशाचमध्ये झोटंगमध्ये डाकिनीमध्ये शंखिनीमध्ये यक्षिणीमध्ये दोषे ीमध्ये शाकिनीमध्ये गुणीमध्ये गारुडीमध्ये विनारीमध्ये दोषमध्ये दोषशरणमध्ये दुष्टमध्ये घोर कष्ट मुझ ऊपरे बुरो जो कोई करावे जड़े जड़ावे तत चिन्ते

चिन्तावे तस माथे श्री माता श्री पंचांगुली देवी वणो वज्र निर्धार पड़े ओ३म् ठं ठं ठं स्वाहा।

कालज्ञान मंत्र:

ओ३म् नमो भगवते ब्रह्मानन्द पद गोलोकादि असंख्या ब्रह्माण्ड भुवन नाथाय शशांक शंक गोक्षीह कर्पूर धवल गात्राय नीलांभोधि जलद पटलाधि-व्यक्तस्व-रूपाय व्याधिकर्म निर्मूलोच्छेदन कराय, जाति जरायुमरण विनाशाय संसारकान्ता रोन्मूलनाय, **अचिन्त्य बल** पराक्रमाय, अतिप्रतिमाह **चक्राय त्रैलोक्याधीश्वराय**, शब्द के त्रैलोक्याधिनरिंवल भुवन कारकाय सर्वसत्य हिताय, निज भक्ताय अभीष्ट फल प्रदाय, भवत्याधीनाय सुरासुरेन्द्रादि मुकुटकोटि घृष्टवाद पीठाय अनन्त युग नाथाय, देवाधिदेवाय, धर्मचक्राधीश्वराय, सर्व विद्या परमेश्वराय, कुविद्याविघ्न प्रदाय, तत्पादपंकजा श्रयानि चवनी देवी सासन देवते त्रिभुवन संक्षोभनी, त्रैलोक्य शिवापहारकरिणीं श्री अद्भुत आतवेदा श्री महालक्ष्मी देवी (अमुकस्य) स्थावर जंगम कृत्रिम विषमुख संहारिणी सर्वाभिचार कर्मापहारिणीं परविद्योछेदनी परमंच प्रनाशिनीं अष्टमहानाग कुलीच्चाटनीं कालदष्टं मृत कोत्यापिनीं (अमुकस्य) सर्वरोग प्रमोचनीं, ब्रह्मा विष्णु रुद्रेन्द्र चन्द्रादित्यादिग्रह नक्षत्रोत्पात मरण भय पीड़ा मर्दिन त्रैलोक्य विश्वलोक वशंकरि, भुविलोक हितकं महाभैरवि शस्त्रोपधारिणीं रौद्र, रौद्ररूप धारी प्रसिद्ध सिद्ध विद्याधर यक्ष राक्षस गरुड़ गन्धर्व किन्नर किं पुरुषो दैत्योरंन्द्र पूजिते ज्वालापात कराल दिगंतराले महावृषभ वाहिनीं, खेटक कृपाण त्रिशूल शक्ति चक्रपाश शरासन शिव विराजमान षोडशार्द्ध भुजे एहि एहि जं ज्वाला मालिनीं हीं हीं त्रुं ह्रीं हीं हं हौं ह: देवान् आकर्षय आकर्षय नाग ग्रहान् आकर्षय आकर्षय यक्ष ग्रहान् आकर्षय आकर्षय गंधर्व ग्रहान आकर्षय आकर्षय ब्रह्मग्रहान् आकर्षय आकर्षय राक्षस ग्रहान् आकर्षय आकर्षय चतुराशि जैन्य मार्ग ग्रहान् आकर्षय आकर्षय चतुर्विंशति जिन ग्रहान् आकर्षय आकर्षय सर्व जटिल ग्रहान् आकर्षय आकर्षय अखिल मुंडित ग्रहान् आकर्षय जंगम ग्रहान् आकर्षय आकर्षय सर्व दुर्गशादि विद्यग्रहान् आकर्षय आकर्षय सर्व नग निग्रह वासी ग्रहान् आकर्षय आकर्षय सर्व जलाशय वासी ग्रहान् आकर्षय आकर्षय सर्व स्थल वासी ग्रहान् आकर्षय आकर्षय सर्वातस्थि ग्रहान् आकर्षय आकर्षय सर्व श्मशान वासी ग्रहान् आकर्षय आकर्षय सर्व पवनी वासी ग्रहान् आकर्षय आकर्षय सर्व धर्म शापादि गौ शाप ग्रहान् आकर्षय आकर्षय सर्व गिरिगुहा दुर्गवासी ग्रहान् आकर्षय आकर्षय श्रापित् ग्रहान् आकर्षय आकर्षय सर्व दुष्ट ग्रहान् आकर्षय आकर्षय वक्र पिंड ग्रहान् आकर्षय आकर्षय कट कट कंपय कंपय शीर्ष चालय शीर्ष चालय गात्रं चालय गात्रं चालय बाहु बाहु चालय पादं चालय कर पल्लवान चालय सर्वांगचालय सर्वांगचालय लोलय धुन धुन कंपय कंपय शीघ्रं भव तारय ग्रहि

ग्रहि ग्राह्य ग्राह्य अक्षय अक्षय आवेशय आवेशय ज्वलूं ज्वालाभालिनीं हां वर्क्रीं व्लूं द्रां द्रां ज्वल ज्वल र र र र र र र र प्रज्वल प्रज्वल धग धग धूमाक्ष करणीं ज्वल विशेषय विशेषय देवग्रहान् दह दह नाग ग्रहान् दह दह यक्ष ग्रहान् दह दह गंधर्व ग्रहान् दह दह ब्रह्म ग्रहान् दह दह राक्षस ग्रहान् दह दह भूत ग्रहान् दह दह दिव्यन्तर ग्रहान् दह दह चतुराशि जैन्य मार्ग ग्रहान् दह दह चतुर्विंश जिन ग्रहान् दह दह सर्व जटिल ग्रहान् दह दह अखिल मुंडित ग्रहान् दह दह जंगम ग्रहान् दह दह सर्व दुर्गशादि विद्या ग्रहान् दह दह सर्व नगनिग्रह वासी ग्रहान दह दह सर्वस्थलवासी ग्रहान् दह दह सर्वान्तरिक्ष वासी ग्रहान् दह दह शमशान वासी ग्रहान् दह दह सर्व गिरिगुहा दुर्गवासी ग्रहान् दह दह श्रापित ग्रहान् दह दह सर्वनाथ पोंथि ग्रहान् दह दह सर्वभूवासी प्रेत ग्रहान् दह दह (अमुक गृहे) असद्गति ग्रहान् दह दह वक्रपिण्ड ग्रहान् दह दह सर्वदुष्ट ग्रहान् दह दह शतकोटि योजने दोषदायी ग्रहान् दह दह सहस्र कोटि योजनान् दोषदायि ग्रहान् दह दह शतकोटि दोष दोष दह दह सहस्रकोटि दोष दह दह आसमुद्राथ् पृथ्वी मध्ये देवभूत पिशाचादि (अमुकस्यो) परिकृत दोषान् तस्य दोषान् दह दह शत्रुकृतभिचार दोषान दह दह धे धे स्फोटय स्फोटय मारय मारय धगि धगि ध गत मुखे ज्वालामालिनी हां हीं हं हैं हौं ह: सर्व ग्रहाणां हृदये दह दह पच पच छिंदि छिंदि भिंदिभिंदि दह दह हा हा स्फुट स्फुट धे धे।

क्ष्म्लुं क्षां क्षीं क्षु क्षैं क्षौं क्ष: स्तंभप: स्तंभप:। भ्भ्लुं भ्रां भ्रीं भ्रुं भ्रैं भ्रौं भ्रं भ्र: बाडय बाडय। भूम्लुं भ्रां भ्रीं भ्रूं भ्रैं भ्रौं भ्र: नेत्रं स्फोटय स्फोटय दर्शय दर्शय। य्म्लुं यां यीं यूं यैं यौं य: प्रेषय प्रेषय। ध्म्लुं ध्रां ध्रीं ध्रूं ध्रैं ध्रौं ध्र: जठेर भेदय। ग्म्लुं ग्रां ग्रीं गुं ग्रैं ग्रौं ग्र: मुखं बंधय। ख्खु-खां-खीं-खु-खैं-खौं-ख: ग्रीवां भंजय भंजय। छप्लुं छां छीं छूं छैं छौं छ: अंत्रान् भेदय भेदय:। द्प्लुं द्रां द्रीं द्रूं द्रौं द्रं। महाविद्युत्पाषाणा स्त्रैहन स्त्रैहन। म्मुं व्रां व्रीं व्रं व्रैं व्रौं व्र: समुद्रे भंजय भंजय। दम्मुं द्रां दुं द्रौं द्र: सर्व डाकिनी सुन्दरी मर्दय मर्दय सर्व योगिनी स्वज्जंय स्वज्जंय। सर्व शत्रु ग्रासय ग्रासय ख ख ख ख ख ख ख खादय खादय सर्व दैत्यान् विध्वंसय विध्वंसय सर्व मृत्युं नाशय नाशय सर्वापद्रवान् स्तंभय स्तंभय ज: ज: ज: ज: ज: ज: ज: ज्वरान् दह दह पच पच घुमु घुमु घुरु घुरु घुरु घुरु घुरु खरु खरु खंग रावण सुविधायां घातय अखिल रुजान् दोषेदयान् कृत कार्यण गाभिचारोत्थान (अमुकस्य) देहे स्थितान् अधुना रुज कारकान् चन्द्रहास शास्त्रेण छेदय छेदय भेदय भेदय उरु उरु छरु छरु स्फुट स्फुट धे आं क्रौं क्षीं क्षं क्षैं क्षौं क्ष: ज्वाला मालिनीं (अमुकस्य) सौख्यं कुरु कुरु निरुजं कुरु कुरु अभिलाषित कामना देहि देहि ज्वाला मालिनीं विज्ञापयते स्वाहा।

◆◆

Practical Knowledge of Palmistry

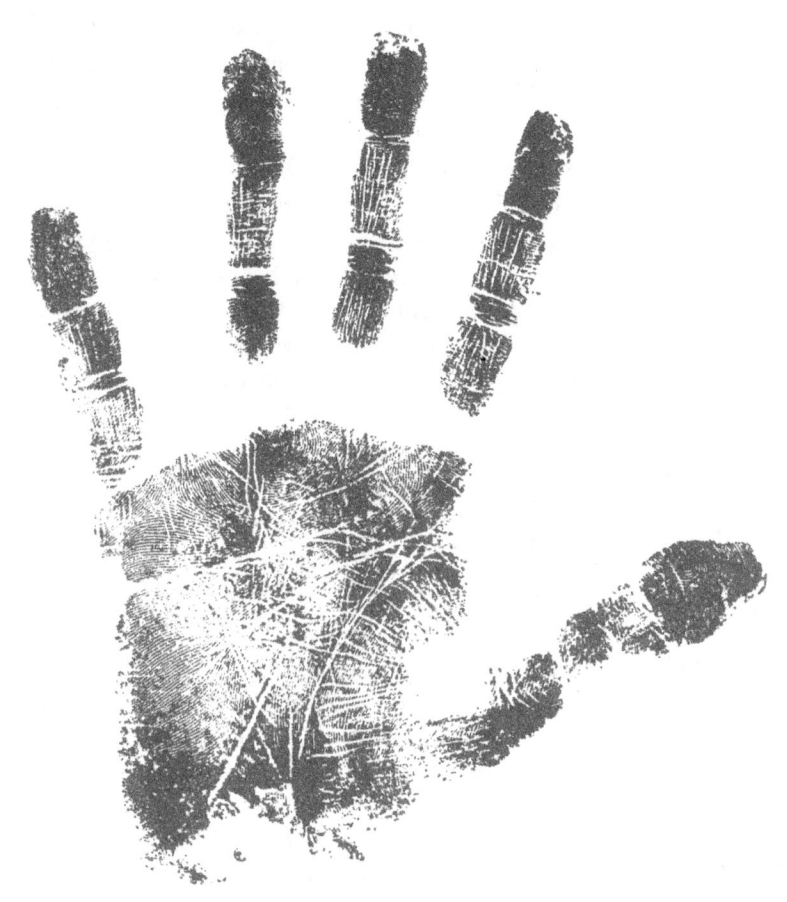

There are facts regarding the lines of hand in the books of Palmistry but none of them has the practical knowledge, due to which the students of Palmistry are able to learn theory of it but have no practical knowledge.

In this book, an attempt is being made for the first time to impart practical knowledge. The hand of an unknown woman was put before Dr. Shrimali. He studied the hand and analysed the following facts :

The hand which was shown to Dr. Shrimali has been printed on this very page. He was sent an imprint of the hand which had neither the name of the woman nor her identity was disclosed to him.

Dr. Shrimali studied the hand and gave a detailed account of it.

Keeping in view the fact that he had given a completely true forecasting, I took my acquaintee, a woman, to his residence and requested him that 1 was coming from the publisher and told him that at the end of his published work, I wanted to give an appendix on practical knowledge of Palmistry. So, Dr. Shrimali should kindly study the lady's hand and give information about it.

Whatever forecast Dr. Shrimali predicted is as follows. Readers should also learn it through Palmistry. The hand-print of the lady is being given here. It is to be kept in view that when the concerned lady and I met Dr. Shrimali, I did not give any information about the lady nor the lady's name, nor did Dr. Shrimali ask us anything about her.

As soon as Dr. Shrimali touched the hand, he said that the mounts of Jupiter, Saturn, Sun and Mercury were fully developed. "It is a tender, soft and ideal hand. It indicates that the lady belongs to a cultured family and that there is a very congenial and civilized atmosphere in her father's as well as her husband's house. The lady is cultured and religious."

"It is a beautiful and fateful hand but the Sun line has been cut, though it is straight. So it indicates that her education is very ordinary. Though there were great efforts to educate her yet she got very ordinary education. At the most, she got education upto class eighth though she appears to be very educated and learned and it appears that she is atleast a graduate. The lines of a hand do not tell lies and it is evident that she got continuous obstructions in her education and so she must have acquired very ordinary education.

On studying the life line, many surprising facts came to light. The initial stage of the life line was that it was formed by many lines. So the first years of the childhood were of illness. "And when one looks minutely, it is deduced that in the 5th year of your life, you suffered from a serious disease but the life line has been cut there and it has relationship with the head line, so it is very clear that there was some trouble and that you nearly escaped death. Isn't it correct?"

The lady nodded in affirmation and replied that she had fallen seriously ill in her fifth year and the members of her family had thought that she would not survive but she got well after a month's illness.

Studying the life line, Dr. Shrimali continued, "It has broken at two or three other places also, so it is also a fact that in the tenth year, there was some special event which took place. This event was like drowning,"

The lady replied, "At the age of ten, I had gone with my mother to a tank and slipped down in deep water. Had I not been saved by the by-standers there, I would have drowned."

Panditji replied that for her future she need not worry. "The future life line is clear and straight and it has reached the bracelets, so there is no possibility of any accident and your full age is nearly 65 or 66 years of age."

"Please wait a minute! Your full age is 65 years, 4 months and 21 days."

The lady smiled gratefully and saw towards Panditji.

"On the life line, there were many lines coming from the mount of Venus and two of them have nearly cut the life line. Along with it, there are many small lines. All these obstructing lines indicate that you had troubles, obstacles and problems. In a way, your childhood was spent in poverty, struggles and troubles. Though your mother line and father line are complete, so they must have longevity, but there cannot be two opinions that your parents did not cooperate in your future life."

"Though I affirm that your parents cooperated in bringing you up but after your marriage, they did not give you support. Isn't it true?"

The lady nodded in affirmative and said nothing. "Now, I am telling you about your age at the time of marriage."

Panditji counted and told her that she was married at a tender age of 14. "On minute examination we know that your marriage line is straight, so you must have spent less part of your life at your parents' house, so as soon as you completed your 14 years, you were married. At the most, it is 14 years and one or two months over it when you were married. I am surprised how you got married at such a tender age? Are early marriages permissible in your society?"

The lady nodded in affirmative and told that she was married when she was 14 years and 1 month old.

Continuing the study of the lines, Panditji said that her husband must have been very ordinary in the beginning, i.e., her inlaw's house was equal in status with her parent's house. Economically and socially, the position of her husband was negligible in the society at the time of their marriage. Her hand contained Girdle of Venus, though it had not formed fully but it indicated that since she went to the house of her husband, she had to face trouble, mental-tensions and anxieties. Physically, she might not have been so perturbed but mentally, she might have suffered tensions and troubles more than enough and she might not have had a respite of even a moment in those days.

The woman nodded in affirmative and asked, "How long will it continue?"

Dr. Shrimali laughed and repeated, "How long?" "It does not mean anything. At that time, she was crossing the age of 42. So that period ended when she was 31 years old. Such mental troubles continued for 15 years after her marriage. From the age of 14 to 31 years, she might have experienced mental tensions. She might not have got respite even for a moment. She did not get any cooperation from her husband then.

But her condition should have improved in her 32nd year of age. By that time, her husband might have established his position in the society and he must have been able to provide her with mental peace, comfort, love, affection and cooperation.

The head line has inclined down and has been cut in the centre, along with it a point is also visible. This point is exactly at the place where the head line has been cut. The period comes to 38th year of her life. So, it seems that she might have received a great mental shock at the 38th year of her life. It seems that she felt darkness all around her and she might have broken down mentally. It appears that from the 32nd year of age to the 38th year of her life, she must have felt her life mentally balanced but that incident must have disturbed her thoroughly. The place where this line has been cut, at that very point, a line coming from the Sun line has met it. So, it appears that the shock received by her might have been from her son. There cannot be two opinions that she received the shock of separation from her eldest son and the incident might have occurred in such a manner that it made her life topsy-turvy. Certainly, the incident indicated the death of her eldest son. The eyes of the lady sitting opposite Panditji were full of tears. She withdrew her hand. She kept silent for a minute or two, then again she stretched her hand before Panditji.

Continuing the study of the line of her palm, he said, "Now, in your future life, you will not face any such incident which may perturb you mentally, though it is true that your mount of Luna is suppressed in itself and is weak which indicates that you will face mental tension throughout. There is always one incident or the other which keeps your mental tensions alive. In my opinion, it will be more suitable for you to wear a pearl in a silver ring and continue to wear it in your future life also. The pearl will be helpful in mitigating your mental problems and troubles.

The lady nodded and inquired as to what sort of pearl she should wear.

Panditji replied, "You should wear the best quality pearl of Basra Lake in Pushya Nakshtra. The pearl should be worn in a silver ring and it will be better if she wears it in the little finger of the right hand."

Panditji continued without moving his head and said, "It seems to me that your health line is chained in initial stage and many smaller lines have emanated out of it but all these lines have moved ahead downward in the palm. It cannot be termed auspicious. These lines indicate this fact that your health must have been very weak and that you must have always suffered from one disease or the other. In fact, right from the 20th year to the 41st year of your life, you must have been in poor health, thereby making it necessary for the doctor to come nearly daily. As in your health line, the last line moving downward indicates the 41st year. All these lines have relationship with the mount of Luna and the mount of Venus. Because of its relationship with the mount of Luna, it seems that your troubles were concerning your stomach including weakness, anaemia, gastric trouble, indigestion, etc. Because of its relationship with the mount of Venus, you might have suffered also from Leucorrhoea and other feminine diseases. Is it true?"

The woman nodded with downcast eyes. "But henceforth, you will not have any trouble from the health point of view, though there may be minor stomach troubles but those also will lessen by wearing a pearl. Your future life seems good from the health point of view. In the 58th year of your life, one more branch has inclined downwards and it has established relationship with the head line, so you will again fall sick for 3 or 4 months at that time."

"In the whole of your future life, you will not have any trouble concerning your health."

"Let me also study your marriage line along with it. As I have already told you, you got favour from your husband at the age of 31 and it is also a fact that your husband must have attained social and economic progress at that time. From the 32nd year, till date you got economic favour and also social favour from your husband. When we study it further, we find that in your future life, your husband will make steady progress economically and socially, and you will get maximum happiness from him. You have no worry in this connection. In truth, no other line is as clear, simple and faultless as this line is. So, there cannot be two opinions that in the whole of your future life, you will get full happiness and honour from your husband. You can be called a very lucky lady that way."

"Now I may also make my views clear on the line of issues, there are six lines visible in your hand. Out of these, four are thick and two are thin. It makes it clear that you will have six issues, out of which four will be sons and two will be daughters. You can yourself see that your first issue line is cut so you will not get happiness of your first issue. As I have already told you, you had to bear the loss of your first issue at the age of 38. In your future life, you will get happiness from three sons and two daughters."

"Along with it, I must tell you that from worldly point of view, you will not lack in happiness from your issues but if you keep this point in view that they will always obey you and will be very obedient, then please remove this illusion from your mind. It is a fact that you have more than enough tolerance, so you will pull on with all of them, though there will be differences and you will have mental agony due to these."

"At the age of 44, you will arrange marriage of a son and a daughter. At the 48th year, you will again arrange the marriage of a son. At the age of 54, a daughter's and at the age of 57, a son's marriage will be arranged by you. You will get special happiness from your present second and third sons. Similarly, your youngest daughter will keep you mentally satisfied the most."

"In your future life, you will have happiness from your issues. Your issues will be capable and they will attain height in their fields. So, from this point of view, you will not be at any loss."

"After counting, it becomes evident that at the age of 47, you will become both grandmother and maternal grandmother. I mean to suggest that you will become a grandmother in that very year."

The woman's face beamed for a moment or two but the next moment she became shy with downcast eyes.

"The mount of Jupiter is the best in itself in your hand, though the Jupiter is inclining towards the Saturn but the mount of Jupiter is faultless and clear. It indicates that you have led a pious life. You incline more towards religious aspects than material aspects of your life. It is your hearty wish that you want to do more and more religious works. You want to serve the cows, the Brahmins and the saints and go on pilgrimages."

"But such is possible only after attaining the age of 36 years. It is also a fact that these religious thoughts will continue in your heart in your future life. As far as possible, you will be able to give alms and will do many other good deeds. Pilgrimages are also likely to continue after the age of 36 years. You will not lack any such thing though due to inclination towards the Saturn, there are always many domestic obstructions. But in one way or the other, these will continue in your life."

"The mount of Saturn is firm on its position and the finger of Saturn has also its full length, so you must be a fortunate woman. You were the cause of progress of your father till you stayed there and you have been the cause of constant progress of your husband since you stepped into his house. I don't feel shy in telling you that the future economic and social progress of your husband will be a clue to the support of your mount of Saturn. So, your husband will continue progressing till he is in your contact or till both of you have congenial relationship. You will also get honour due to it."

"The mount of Sun is also strong in your hand, but it has inclined towards the mount of Saturn and also the line of Sun is composed of many other lines. (Though the allied lines provide force to the line of the Sun but some of these lines are cutting it as well). So it is obvious in your life that you may do whatever amount of work, you will not get any credit for it. If I may tell you the truth, you did not get any credit at your father's house nor did you get any credit at your in-laws' house. Though it is a fact that you will always serve everybody in your in-law's family, you will also help them from time to time. You will also keep sweet and favourable behaviour with them. But when need be, you will neither get any cooperation nor any credit from them. By studying your hand, it is clear that you got your father-in-law's love for 14 years after your marriage but your mother-in-law has longevity. But there cannot be two opinions that you got obstructions, troubles, obstacles and mental tensions from them. The more you tried to give them pleasures and happinesses, the more they troubled you physically and mentally. This fact is also true with your brother-in-law, sister-in-law, mother-in-law, your brother and your parents. What I mean to suggest is that you will always try to help them but they will not give you any credit nor any honour, nor will you find these from them in your future life.

Instead, you will go on helping them and will try to give them comfort and happiness till you die.

You must have noted it in your hand that one line starts from the mount of Jupiter and meets the line of Sun. So, whatever cooperation and honour you will get, it will be from your husband. You will get the love and cooperation of your husband throughout your life and this fact will mitigate your mental tensions.

So far as the mount of Mercury is concerned, it is generally good. But it has enlarged outside your palm and also the line of Mercury has enlarged towards the little finger. It makes it clear that you are a minute observer and a wise lady. This is also true that you can understand the true character of any unknown person or any lady, also his standard and whether he will be helpful or not. All these things are clear in your mind in the fraction of a second. You might have also felt that whatever you think about them proves to be quite true.

Along with it, this mount of Mercury informs that you are endowed with the godly gift that many times you know about the coming events beforehand and you might have also felt that those events were quite true. It is because of your pure and sinless heart. This fact also reveals that you are a blessed one. On this mount of Mercury, one line meets it (coming from the mount of the Moon). So, there is a clear indication of your visit abroad. The fate line relationship is also clear here. So, you may go abroad in the 41st, 43rd and 46th years of your life. The last two visits out of these will be important and favourable. Most of these will be with your husband but in the 56th year, you may go abroad with your son.

You will be able to see most of Europe and parts of America by these visits. Whereas the duration of the visits is 1 to 4 months, these will be beneficial to you from the health (both mental and physical) point of view.

You will also visit the whole of India in your life and will proceed on pilgrimages many times in your life.

The mount of Moon is constrained and is slipping inside the palm. So, this mount will give you mental tension and troubles. As I have already told you, you will keep on suffering from gastric trouble and indigestion, etc. Whatever mental tensions you have sufferred, the main reason for them was the mount of Moon on your palm. I have already given you the remedy for it earlier.

The Dragon's Head is suppressed in your hand. It is a favour in itself. It has not allowed you to have irreligious or immoral thoughts and feelings, nor is it possible in your future life. In a way, its suppression has helped in giving height to your religious feelings.

The bracelets are favourable for you. The first bracelet is chained which gives profits. The three bracelets in your hand give you longevity.

The mount of Venus is also favourable. The life line is bow-shaped and it has given dimensions to the mount of Venus. The obstructing lines on it indicate obstacles in your life about which I have already informed you. The mount of Venus has protruded near the palm which indicates that there is a happy combination of material and spiritual devotion. In a way, the tendencies of pleasure have a special effect of religious tendencies in your life and it is favourable in your life."

"Your thumb has full length and is drawn back. It shows your firmness of will. This thumb also indicates that you remain firm on your views in your life. Once whatever you decide, you try to fulfil it, come what may."

"The first phalange of the thumb is long and firm in itself. This firmness helps in developing logic in you. It also appears that you do not work with closed eyes, instead you either rectify it or try to give it newness. By looking at this phalange of your thumb, it appears that you like criticism of others a little. If a work has been done by anyone other than you, then either you will try to find fault in it or you will not hesitate in giving this suggestion that the work would have been done better the other way.

The root of the thumb, where the mount of Venus has started developing, is protruded. The protrusion leads you towards materialism. It has been your innermost feeling to live grandly and decently. You also have a little love for exhibition in your heart.

A horizontal line from the mount of Venus has gone to the mount of Mars. It has cut all the obstructing lines. If we compare it with your age line, then it comes to the age of 43. Mars is the owner of land and Venus is that of material happiness. Therefore, it so seems that by the end of the 43rd year and at the beginning of the 44th year of your life, you will have your own house. It is different that you neither serve anywhere nor do you have any independent source of income, but this ownership of house will be possible by the wealth and cooperation of your husband.

There is a rectangle near the line of Mars at the 37th year of age. There was possibility of house building or of purchasing land at that time. But it seems that the house could not be constructed then, only land was possibly purchased. In my opinion, this land was purchased by you or by someone else in your name."

"The line of Mars in your hand is very strong and it goes parallel to the life line. Because of the developed mount of Mars, you must have the feeling of somewhat great anger. It appears that you are more than enough watchful about your personality. As and when your ego or self-respect gets hurt, then you become very angry. At that time, you begin washing dirty linens of your antagonist and it is your tendency to make your point of view firm and strong. To make it so, you indulge in all sorts of activities and logic which favour you. Along with it, as already told by me that the line of Mars goes parallel to the life line, it puts self-confidence in you. You must have more than enough self-confidence. You do not get nervous by any sort of obstacle instead. You console your aquaintees during their days of calamity and help them in swimming over their seas of troubles. This is your bright side.

From the mount of Mars, one line has gone to the mount of Saturn and it appears that though it has not touched the fate line, it has certainly reached near it. So it can be assumed that you will not get any benefit from land deals in future."

"It is my humble advice that you should not go for any land deals in your name. It will be appropriate and favourable for you.

All the other minor lines in your hand are generally favourable. The life line, head line and health line combine to form a triangle. Sometimes the line of Moon also provides this triangle a shape. This triangle is favourable in itself. This triangle clearly indicates that the later half of your life is more favourable and full of happiness. Broadly speaking, if we assume your whole life span as of 68 years, then your favourable period started after the 34th year of your life. This favour and hapiness will continue in your future life. In my opinion, you should worship Lord Vishnu or Lord Krishna to get favour in your life. Besides, the worship of Lord Ram, Goddess Laxmi and other gods and goddesses will help you to get favour."

The lady raised her head and said, "Panditji, whatever you have said till now is all true but I want to know the answers of some of my questions."

Panditji replied, "Please ask me without hesitation. I do not have any objection to it."

The lady smiled and said, "You can know the month of birth by reading one's palm and you can also make out the exact day, date and time of birth through it. I am still in doubt about it. My mother did not remember the exact time of my birth. Sometimes, she tells one time, another time another. There is difference of two to three hours in both the timings.

Panditji replied, "It is not difficult to correct the time of birth through Palmistry. Please wait a minute, I will resolve your problem just now."

Panditji took out the magnifying glass and studied the lines of palm. He said, "You must be born in April because on the second phalange of the finger of Saturn, there is only one complete line, rest all the lines are broken and faint. If we calculate the date, then by counting the lines, it comes to 8th day of April."

Waiting for a few moments, Panditji said, "Certainly you were born on April 8th, 1933. So far as the date of birth is concerned, it is verified through reading the line of the palm, you remember the exact date of your birth."

"Yes Panditji, you have correctly told me the date of my birth through studying the lines of palm. My date of birth is really April 8th, 1933."

Fixing his eyes on the palm, Panditji further said, "So far as the study of first phalange of your thumb is concerned, it clearly indicates that your sign of zodiac should be cancer and this is just more than two degrees. Thus, your birth time should be about 24 seconds at thirty-one minutes past eight in the evening. This time when calculated, tells that the zodiac of Cancer has past only two degrees.

Your forecast seems to be true because my mother has told me the time between 7 P.M. and 10 P.M. The astrologer who prepared my horoscope has done it with the sign of zodiac as Cancer but he has calculated it as past eight degrees. It seems that he did not know the exact time of my birth. Whatever past events you have told me are fully correct and on that basis, in my opinion, the time told by you is the correct one and the most authentic one."

Panditji said slowly, "Please consider it fully authentic. Whatever time I have told is true because if one prepares your horoscope on its basis and ascertains the signs of zodiac, then it corroborates with the lines of your palm. Thus, the incidents which became clear by reading the lines of your palm can also be indicated by reading your horoscope." Waiting for a few moments, Panditji further said, "In a moment, I may also give you a clear picture of the position of different planets when you were born. The sign of zodiac (Lagna) in your horoscope should be Cancer and in the Leo, there should be confluence of your planets with the Leo, the Jupiter, the Moon, the Mars and the Dragon's Tail. In the same way, in the house of Capricorn, there should be Saturn, in Aquarius, there should be Dragon's Head and in Pisces, there should be Sun, Mercury and Venus (all the three to be seated together). In fact, this is the real composition of your horoscope."

The woman brought out her horoscope from her bag and on perusal found that the same was the position of planets in it, i.e., the one told by Panditji was true.

Concluding the study of her hand, Panditji told her the following more facts :

1. You do not have any such line in your hand by virtue of which you may get sudden wealth. Neither have you got sudden wealth till now nor will you get it in your future.
2. You have got the comfort of a vehicle in the beginning of your 44th year of age. It will be a car and it will continue in your future life.

3. Economically, you do not have any problem or obstacles in your future life.
4. You have conchshell marks on your little finger and a mark of mountain on your index finger is there. So the last half of your life is favourable and full of happiness.
5. You have clearly the Laxmi Yog, Brahm Yog, Sadhu Yog, Maha Laxmi Yog, Kalakar Yog, Pativrata Yog, Kailash Yog Kamal Yog and I have described all these combinations in detail in this very book entitled *Practical Palmistry*. You can look for facts regarding these in the book.
6. The whole of your future life will be favourable and full of happiness from spiritual point of view. You will die due to heart attack in your house amongst the members of your family and you will die before the death of your husband which is an ideal for an Indian woman.

The woman was fully impressed by the knowledge of Panditji. She got up and touched his feet and said, "The analysis made by you after reading my hand is completely true and fully authentic. Your knowledge in Palmistry is surprising. I have reverence for you and your deep knowledge."

Panditji replied, "I am not very important in it. We should show reverence and be modest to our ancient literature, our knowledge of Palmistry and our ancestor monks who gave us this knowledge. I am just a means. I only light the lamp of knowledge given by them so that in its light more and more people can find their way; thereby they may make their lives favourable and orderly and may get fullness from all aspects of life."

"Keeping in view these aims, I have established the *Bhartiya Jyotish Anusandhan Kendra at High Court Colony, Jodhpur (Rajasthan)* and I have engaged the best pandits here so that people living in India and abroad may get guidance through the study of horoscopes and the study of lines of the palms for their future benefits."

"I am glad to note that the centre has earned reputation and fame in a very short time. Today, here we get thousands of palmprints and horoscopes for study from India and abroad. All are satisfied here and all have praised the work here."

"I believe this centre will definitely be able to represent India in the field of astrology."   ◆◆

Conclusion

Every human being or creature has a part of God and hence, we are called the sons of God. God has all done it orderly and with understanding. If you have been created, then there is mystery in its background or there may be a great necessity. In fact, your creation is only your creation in the whole of the universe. There is none like you in the whole world. It is possible that some are better than you and others are worse than you but the proportion of ingredients in 'you' is solitary. So it is said that the lines in your hand are your own lines. No two persons in the world can have similar lines. Therefore, all individuals have individuality of personality. God has spread the whole world before you. Now it depends upon you what sort of place should you have and how to create such a place for yourself in this world. For this, it is to be seen how you utilize the moments of your life. Every moment is a moment of gift bestowed on you by God. The moment passed can't come back, though we might spent crores to get it back.

When one moment is more valuable than lakhs and crores of rupees, then you have no authority to spend it carelessly or in useless discussions or in useless activities. You should think that every moment of your life has utility and you have to utilize every moment accurately. It depends upon you that how you cope up with those moments yourself and the world around you. This world is constantly moving and if you also move along with it, you will definitely develop but if your speed is less than the speed of progress of the world, then you will lag behind and the world will go ahead of you. After that, though you do great efforts, you can't cope up with the speed of the moving world.

This whole life is your own. All the moments of life are open before you. You should use even the smallest moment. Recognize every opportunity and close it into your fist. Try to experience the heartbeat of even a moment of the future time and try to make it in your favour. It is in your hand and if you do that, you will see that the lines of your palm are changing and rising above and your steps are moving towards progress, success, honour and fame. What you need is to proceed forward and to accept the garlands which are waiting for you eagerly.

Every work of life has two aspects: the positive and the negative. We can analyse any work in these two aspects or we can say that we are standing between creation and destruction. It depends upon you whether you create the moments of your life or you destroy them. In fact, you are not dead but you are alive, active and moving and keep every moment moving. Your feet should constantly move towards progress.

You should get up, be active and be creative. Be assured that the all-round wide gulf of have nots and frustration will end itself. The thorns of the path will turn into flowers. But it will require self-confidence, courage, a daring attitude and patience. You need a will to move ahead constantly.

You have the time, energy, labour, health and life. Use them with both of your hands. Whatever energy and time you have got, the same was also with Gandhi, Tagore, Tolstoy, Lincoln and Jesus. Then what is the reason that they are still shining like stars in the world and you are wandering in wilderness anonymously. Why are you lagging behind? Why are you tottering? Get up and move ahead, success is before you, victory is calling you. Fame and honour are waiting to welcome you and sucess is standing with a garland to choose you.

Fill your heart and nerve with courage and move ahead. Each of your steps should be firm. Your sight should be able to see the other surface of a thing. It is in your hands to change your weak lines and turn your misfortune into luck. It is time for you to work; your time begins now and it is the call of time of your life.

SELF-IMPROVEMENT/PERSONALITY DEVELOPMENT

   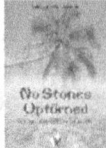    

Also Available in Hindi   Also Available in Hindi   Also Available in Kannada, Tamil

Also Available in Kannada

Also Available in Kannada

    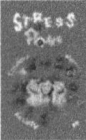   

STRESS MANAGEMENT

All books available at www.vspublishers.com

RELIGION/SPIRITUALITY/ASTROLOGY/PALMISTRY/PALMISTRY/VASTU/HYPNOTISM

CAREER & BUSINESS MANAGEMENT

Also Available in Hindi, Kannada

Also Available in Hindi, Kannada

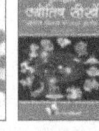 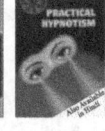   

Contact us at sales@vspublishers.com

QUIZ BOOKS

ENGLISH IMPROVEMENT

     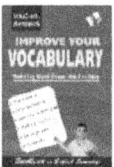 

ACTIVITIES BOOK

QUOTES/SAYINGS

BIOGRAPHIES

CHILDREN SCIENCE LIBRARY

IELTS TECH

Set Code: 02122 8   Set Code: 12138 S

COMPUTER BOOKS

Also available in Hindi   Also available in Hindi

All books available at www.vspublishers.com

www.ingramcontent.com/pod-product-compliance
Lightning Source LLC
Chambersburg PA
CBHW070645160426
43194CB00009B/1583